Understanding the Te Whāriki Approach is a much-needed source of information for those wishing to extend and consolidate their understanding of the Te Whāriki approach, introducing the reader to an innovative bicultural curriculum developed for early childhood services in New Zealand. It will enable the reader to analyse the essential elements of this approach to early childhood and its relationship to quality early years practice.

Providing students and practitioners with the relevant information about a key pedagogical influence on high quality early years practice in the UK, the book explores all areas of the curriculum, emphasising:

- strong curriculum connections to families and the wider community;
- a view of teaching and learning that focuses on responsive and reciprocal relationships with people, places and things;
- a view of curriculum content as cross-disciplinary and multi-modal;
- the aspirations for children to grow up as competent and confident learners and communicators, healthy in mind, body and spirit, secure in their sense of belonging and in the knowledge that they make a valued contribution to society;
- a bicultural framework in which indigenous voices have a central place.

Written to support the work of all those in the field of early years education and childcare, this is a vital text for students, early years and childcare practitioners, teachers, early years professionals, children's centre professionals, lecturers, advisory teachers, head teachers and setting managers.

Wendy Lee is the Project Director of the Educational Leadership Project, which provides professional development for early childhood teachers in Aotearoa New Zealand.

Margaret Carr is Professor of Education at the University of Waikato, Aotearoa New Zealand, and was one of the Directors of the curriculum development project that developed Te Whāriki.

Brenda Soutar is a Kaitiaki (Leader) at Mana Tamariki, an education setting that nurtures and teaches children from 0–17 years through total immersion in the Māori language and learning environments in their kōhanga reo (early childhood setting), kura kaupapa Māori (primary school) and wharekura (secondary school).

Linda Mitchell is an Associate Professor and early childhood education policy analyst at the University of Waikato, Aotearoa New Zealand.

Understanding the . . . Approach
Series Editors: Pat Brunton and Linda Thornton

This new series provides a much needed source of information for those wishing to extend and consolidate their understanding of international approaches to early years education and childcare. The books will enable the reader to analyse the essential elements of each approach and its relationship to quality early years practice.
Each book:

■ Describes the key principles of the approach to early childhood with practical examples and case studies;
■ Provides students and practitioners with the relevant information about a key pedagogical influence on high quality early years practice;
■ Highlights the key ideas that practitioners should consider when reviewing and reflecting on their own practice;
■ Can be used as the basis for continuing professional development and action research

Written to support the work of all those in the field of early years education and childcare, these will be invaluable texts for students, early years and childcare practitioners, teachers, early years professionals, children's centre professionals, lecturers, advisory teachers, head teachers and setting managers.

Understanding the
Te Whāriki Approach

Early Years Education
in Practice

Wendy Lee, Margaret Carr,
Brenda Soutar and Linda Mitchell

Routledge
Taylor & Francis Group

LONDON AND NEW YORK

First published 2013
by Routledge
2 Park Square, Milton Park, Abingdon, Oxon OX14 4RN

Simultaneously published in the USA and Canada
by Routledge
711 Third Avenue, New York, NY 10017

Routledge is an imprint of the Taylor & Francis Group, an informa business

British Library Cataloguing in Publication Data
A catalogue record for this book is available from the British Library

Library of Congress Cataloging in Publication Data
Understanding the Te Whariki approach : early years education in
practice / Wendy Lee . . . [et al.].
     p. cm.
  1. Early childhood education–New Zealand. 2. Multicultural
  education–New Zealand. I. Lee, Wendy (Early childhood
  education professional) II. Title.
  LB1139.3.N45U53 2012
  372.210993–dc23   2012026707

ISBN: 978–0–415–61712–3 (hbk)
ISBN: 978–0–415–61713–0 (pbk)
ISBN: 978–0–203–07534–0 (ebk)

Typeset in Palatino and Futura
by Swales & Willis Ltd, Exeter, Devon

MIX
Paper from
responsible sources
FSC
www.fsc.org   FSC® C004839

Printed and bound in Great Britain by
TJ International Ltd, Padstow, Cornwall

Contents

Figures

Tables

Acknowledgements and introduction

Our first acknowledgement is to Routledge for inviting Wendy to contribute to their Approach series. Wendy responded by gathering together a thinking and writing team with a mixture of interests and expertise. Margaret brings a background of early childhood teaching and an interest in and knowledge of researching curriculum and pedagogy; Brenda brings cultural knowledge and experience as a kaitiaki (teacher) at a kōhanga reo, and is also a writer, researcher and professional development provider; Linda brings expertise in researching and evaluating policy and quality early childhood environments. Wendy's knowledge and experience in teaching and professional development has resulted in her and the Educational Leadership Project team responding to teachers' requests for guidance and inspiration in many early childhood contexts and in many countries beyond Te Whāriki's home country, New Zealand.

We have all participated in action research with teachers in the Ministry's Centre of Innovation programme, which ran for 7 years from 2002 to 2009, and short case studies or commentaries from six Centres of Innovation projects in which the authors have participated are included in this book (Greerton Early Childhood Centre, Wadestown Kindergarten, Te Kōhanga Reo o Mana Tamariki, Wilton Playcentre, Roskill South Kindergarten and Mangere Bridge Kindergarten). So our second acknowledgement is to the Ministry of Education for initiating and funding this teacher research programme—and, in retrospect, for enabling what was at the time an unusual curriculum approach to become a key platform for early childhood teachers' work. We are grateful too, for those in the Ministry, especially Mary Chamberlain, who led the 2007 New Zealand school curriculum development that has included a curriculum pathway from Te Whāriki into school.

The New Zealand Council for Educational Research (NZCER) has administered another teacher research programme on behalf of the Ministry: the Teaching and Learning Research Initiative (TLRI). Many early childhood teachers, as researchers, have benefited directly and indirectly from this initiative. NZCER Press has also published work by and for teachers in their journals designed for teachers: Early Childhood Folio and SET. These journals are now published online and continue to provide ideas and inspiration to teachers in New Zealand and across the globe. It is one of the viewpoints in this book, especially expressed in Chapter 9, that all good teachers—qualified and unqualified—are researching their practice from day to day as they observe and interact with children and try to work out how best to provide a responsive environment. This Routledge Series contributes ideas and reflective questions to assist with that research. The document, Te Whāriki, too, includes 111 reflective questions with (in our view) teachers as researchers in mind.

Any curriculum approach is useful only if teachers make the ideas their own by adapting and recontextualising them in their own context. Children have to do this too, and teachers notice them doing it. We have often talked with teachers about a curriculum filter: *noticing, recognising and responding*, a sequence that Bronwen Cowie brought to our attention from the field of assessment in secondary school classrooms. Teachers notice a lot, and some of what they notice will be recognised as learning of interest. Teaching is a complex task and they can only respond to some of what is recognised as being of interest. Teachers who read and talk about teaching ideas and practices can enhance the efficiency of the filter: they notice more, recognise more and have more practices for a ready response. We have added *recording* and *revisiting* to this filter now, and the same increase in efficiency from reading and reflecting applies.

N O T I C I N G

RECOGNISING

RESPONDING

RECORDING

REVISITING

During the writing of this book a number of international colleagues have written to comment on the influence of Te Whāriki and its implementation in their country. We have included some of these comments— from England, Germany, Denmark, the USA, and Australia – at the head of Chapters 1, 2, 3, 8, 9 and 10. Our thanks for these comments go to Margy Whalley (Pen Green Research, Development & Training Base and Leadership Centre, Corby, England), Sibylle Haas (Eigenbetrieb Kindertagesstätten Nordwest, Berlin, Germany), Margie Carter (Harvest Resources Associates, Seattle, USA), Trish Tranfa (Eastern Adelaide region, Department for Education and Child Development, Australia), Jenny Woodbridge (former Director, Early Excellence Training and Resource Centre, Huddersfield, England), Norah Waugh (Education Development Service, Durham Local Authority, England), Stig Broström (The Research Unit of Childhood, Learning and Curriculum Studies, Aarhus University, Copenhagen, Denmark), and Mark Whitney (Faculty of Child Development, MiraCosta College, California, USA).

We also want to thank the teachers who so willingly provided us with comments and learning stories; we regret that we have not been able to include them all. Teachers' comments head up Chapters 4, 5, 6 and 7, and other comments, photographs, conversations and learning stories are woven throughout the book. These contributions come from:

- Albany Kindergarten
- Carol White Children and Family Centre
- Greerton Early Childhood Centre
- Pakuranga Baptist Kindergarten
- Pigeon Mountain Kindergarten
- Roskill South Kindergarten
- Samoa Taumafi Aoga Amata
- Selwyn Kindergarten
- Stanmore Bay Kindergarten
- Tai Tamariki Kindergarten
- Taupo Kids Community
- Te Kōhanga Reo o Mana Tamariki

Thanks so much to Zach Morton-Jones, who drew the animal pictures that appear throughout the book. His mother, Sarah, sent a commentary on the context of the drawings:

> One day Zach went to the zoo with his Dad and sisters. When he got back home from the zoo, he went straight to his drawing table where he always keeps a mountain of paper and pens. He looked very serious as he began to draw. He sat there, very busy, drawing for a long time. When he had finished his drawings

he went running to Dad. 'Look at all the animals I drew!!!' Zach had drawn every
animal he could remember seeing at the zoo. He was very proud of his pictures.

The drawings, therefore, not only represent a decorative addition to
the chapters; they also represent some features of learning that is valued
in the Te Whāriki approach: intense interest, a deep focus on personalised
meaning-making, pride in achievement as an artist (a possible self), a
reciprocal relationship between the centre and a family who is willing to
share their child's experience at home, and a teacher who values that
experience enough to ask permission to send it to a researcher, Wendy.
We hope that readers will appreciate, want to talk about and be willing to
experiment with, these and other aspects of early years education in
practice described in this book.

The plan for this book

Chapter 1 sets the historical and cultural stage for the development
of a national early childhood curriculum. Chapter 2 introduces the development of Te Whāriki, including key theoretical positioning. Chapter 3
describes the bicultural and bilingual underpinning of Te Whāriki, and
some of the implications for practice of this.

Chapters 4 to 7 individually consider the four principles. Each of
these four chapters begins with a reflection from a teacher, includes a
table that suggests the ways in which the principle is reflected in learning
outcomes, and adds a case study analysis of how the five strands are
emphasised in four individual early childhood education settings: an
education and care centre (Chapter 4), a kindergarten (Chapter 5), a
kōhanga reo (Chapter 6) and a playcentre (Chapter 7).

Chapter 8 puts the weaving back together, returning to the 'responsive
and reciprocal relationships' principle by emphasising three aspects of a
curriculum environment: the goals, the assessment and the planning.

Chapter 9 describes the teacher as a researcher and considers the ways
in which the implementation of Te Whāriki has enabled teachers to
continue to learn, and enabled the curriculum to remain open-ended,
and what lessons we might gain from this.

Chapter 10 asks 'What next?' A number of chapters (as this one did)
include a learning and teaching episode, sometimes a learning story,
written by a teacher, that illustrates some aspect of the discussion and is
designed to spark and sustain dialogue amongst readers.

1 Setting the stage for Te Whāriki

From England, Margy Whalley writes:

Cultural defamiliarisation (Tobin, 2009 p.159) has been extremely important for those of us working at Pen Green, a fully integrated centre for children and their families. Several of our original team, the pioneers who set up the centre in 1983, had worked in majority world cultures, had experience of a range of pedagogical approaches and had worked in diverse settings in this country and overseas. When staff began to visit nurseries in Denmark and Italy in the 1990s we learnt to appreciate just how much of what was taken for granted in the UK as being 'good practice' in Early Years provision was culturally determined. It was not until we visited New Zealand 10 years later that we felt we had found a curriculum framework and pedagogical approach that really made sense to children, families and practitioners. We were lucky enough to work with powerful colleagues from New Zealand who shared unreservedly the emerging Te Whāriki framework in all its different stages. We loved the fact that the framework was an emerging document, co-constructed at every step with practitioners, written in an engaging style but with lyrical prose and focusing on the things we thought were absolutely critical: a bicultural approach, an approach that focused on the child within the family context and with a central concern for children's dispositions to learn. We owe our New Zealand colleagues a debt of gratitude for the powerful materials that they have produced. The Te Whāriki curriculum has had a huge impact on practice in our setting and across the UK.

Introduction

Each of the books in this Routledge 'Understanding' series so far has described approaches to early childhood education (ECE) that link theory to pedagogy in a particular practice. This book describes an example of an early childhood *national curriculum*, Te Whāriki, that makes these links. It is also an official description of young learners with an explicit view about the nation in which they will become citizens. This book therefore has three tasks to enable the reader to begin the journey of understanding Te Whāriki. The first of these is to set out the contextual, cultural and historical features that underpinned and influenced the development and implementation of Te Whāriki as the national early childhood curriculum for Aotearoa New Zealand.[1] The second task is to describe the principles, pedagogies and early childhood practices that have arisen from those features. The third task is to signal the ways in which some of those principles, pedagogies and early childhood practices can be recontextualised so that they might become interesting and useful for discussions about early childhood practice elsewhere. All three tasks or agendas are interwoven through the book.

The aim of this Routledge series, as we see it, is to provoke dialogue, debate and experimentalism (Moss, 2009). In Aotearoa New Zealand we are still exploring new ways to implement Te Whāriki, and we hope in this book to provide enough material for lively discussions about the ways that this approach can inform short, medium and long-term practices and visions here and elsewhere. This chapter introduces the first of the above three tasks: setting out the contextual, cultural and historical features that underpin and influence the development and implementation of Te Whāriki. At the end of the chapter we invite readers to contemplate these features of their own curriculum.

New Zealand's history is important for an understanding of Te Whāriki

Aotearoa New Zealand is a small, geographically remote island country located in the southern Pacific Ocean. It was the last country in the world to be discovered and settled. Eastern Polynesian migrants came in canoe groups probably in the thirteenth century AD, although some historians put the date earlier than this (King, 2003). Māori were the first settlers and are the indigenous people of Aotearoa New Zealand. It was not until 1769, after its rediscovery by British Royal Navy Lieutenant James Cook, that Europeans set foot on the land and soon after began settling here.

With a population of 4.5 million it is similar in size to Finland (5.5 million) and Singapore (5 million), countries whose school reforms have been of interest in the educational world (Luke, 2011; Sahlberg, 2010). Allan Luke comments on the relative success of these curriculum models (including Ontario, Canada):

> The stories of Singapore, Finland, and Ontario are not about the triumph of scientific methods. They are not about the triumph of markets, or successful standardization. They are about cultural and governmental settlements, about durable historical, social, and cultural commitments to particular forms of education and, indeed, forms of life (Luke, 2011 p.374).

There are some features of these settlements and commitments in the Te Whāriki story, and the historical, social and cultural history of Aotearoa New Zealand is relevant to an understanding. This country had become a self-governing democracy in 1856 and in 1893 was the first in the world to give women the vote. It was called the social laboratory of the world for its welfare state policies following the Great Depression of the 1930s. These values are reflected in Te Whāriki's focus on equity and respect for children's rights (and responsibilities), together with the aim of supporting children growing up in a democracy in which they will make a contribution. The aspiration statement at the beginning of the document says that 'The curriculum is founded on the following aspirations for children: To grow up as competent and confident learners and communicators, healthy in mind, body and spirit, secure in their sense of belonging and in the knowledge that they make a valued contribution to society'.

The curriculum looks ahead to citizens who can make responsible and informed choices, respect the ideas and beliefs of others, include diversity in their world-view and have an understanding of both major cultures and languages of the country. The treaty between Māori and the British Crown, Te Tiriti o Waitangi, signed in 1840 (see Chapter 3) was to provide the foundation for a country with three official languages, Māori, English and NZ Sign, and a vision of a bicultural society. Te Whāriki is a bilingual document in English and Māori. Valuing and promoting diversity and upholding Māori rights to tino rangatiratanga (authority over their lives and resources) can be seen both in the story of the development of Te Whāriki and the story of the growth of early childhood care and education (ECCE) provision in Aotearoa New Zealand. A theme of this book is that the Te Whāriki approach is not a series of strategies or outcomes that can be taken on elsewhere without a close look at the social and cultural infrastructure that supports and surrounds early childhood services. New Zealand has had a tradition of social welfare policies with a vision of equity and opportunity, a bicultural treaty with

Māori that includes te reo as a 'taonga' (treasure),[2] a commitment to public education and a cultural belief in the power of creativity and improvisation: early settlers – Māori, Pākehā (see glossary) and migrants from Pacific island nations – adapted to a very different environment in innovative and skilful ways. Early European immigrants in the nineteenth century could shrug off some of the class constraints of 'home' to develop hybrid identities that included new opportunities for crafting their own life journeys.

Diversity of services

The stories of early childhood in Aotearoa New Zealand are eloquently told by Helen May, and readers will find in her histories – *The Discovery of Early Childhood* (1997), *Politics in the Playground* (2009), and *I Am Five and I Go to School* (2011) – a wealth of stories and details that make the history come alive and position early childhood inside the wider lenses of education, society and culture, internationally and nationally.

A diversity of ECE provision preceded the development of Te Whāriki. ECE in Aotearoa New Zealand covers the period from birth to school starting age (usually at the age of 5 years, but compulsory at the age of 6). The various and distinctive types of early childhood services mostly developed from community and parent initiatives in response to a particular need within their social and political context. In the last two decades this strong community basis has shifted somewhat as a growing number of business owners have set up centre-based or home-based childcare services. The diversity of provision and freedom of philosophy has been staunchly upheld in Aotearoa New Zealand. Enabling multiple curricula within a common framework also became one of the aims in the curriculum development process. Recently, for policy purposes, the ECE services have been categorised broadly as teacher-led and parent/whānau-led to differentiate between how the services operate and are funded. These are briefly introduced below.

Teacher-led services

A teacher-led service is one where one or more qualified teachers are responsible for the overall programme in the service. They are required to have a person responsible who is a registered, ECE qualified teacher and meets the government's teacher registration targets. All teacher-led services are working towards a policy of an 80% qualified (with the equivalent of a 3-year degree or diploma) teaching team. Education and care centres (childcare centres) cater for the largest number of children and offer full day, sessional or half day provision. These cater for children from birth to the school starting age. Chapter 4 includes a case study of Te Whāriki in an education and care centre. Kindergartens have traditionally been sessional services for 3-year-old and 4-year-old children. Many are now expanding their hours in response to community needs, including those of working women, and funding incentives; they have moved recently to school day or full day provision and often include children under 3 years of age. Chapter 5 includes a case study of Te Whāriki in a kindergarten.

Home-based services (family daycare) tend to be flexible, providing an educator to work with children in the educator's home or the child's home at hours to suit parents. The correspondence school is a distance service and the only one that is directly provided by the state.

Parent/whānau-led services

Kōhanga reo (Māori immersion language nests) were established in 1982 and have been described as 'the most vigorous and innovative educational movement in this country (dare I say in the world)' (Reedy, 2003, p.65). These offer total immersion in Māori and are managed by whānau (the extended family). The kōhanga reo philosophy centres on fostering Māori language and cultural identity as well as self-determination. A core aim is 'passing on the Māori way of life to future generations' (Government Review Team, 1988, p.19). Most kōhanga reo operate for 30 or more hours per week. Chapter 3 tells more of this story, and Chapter 6 provides a case study of Te Whāriki in a kōhanga reo.

Playcentres are a uniquely New Zealand service and based on a belief in the family as the most important setting for the care and education of the child. Developed during the Second World War (Somerset, 1976a, 1976b) as a support for mothers, parents undertake all roles, including curriculum implementation, management and administration. Parents are provided with playcentre training, which is education designed to enhance the parents' understanding of human development and their role as educators of their children (Hill et al., 2000). Chapter 7 includes a case study of Te Whāriki in a playcentre. Sessional playgroups are also run by parents, but they require no training, unlike in playcentres. They are usually small, often operating in community halls. Playgroups include Māori immersion and community language playgroups for different ethnic communities, as well as general playgroups.

Pacific early childhood groups offer total immersion or bilingual education in their home Pacific language. They may be sessional or full day. These services arose mainly from a desire by Pacific women to ensure that their Pacific languages and traditions were passed on to succeeding New Zealand-born generations (Mitchell *et al.*, 2006, p.43). They may be staffed by qualified teachers and in those cases are termed 'teacher-led'. A'oga Fa'a Samoa, a Samoan early childhood centre, was initiated by Samoan grandparents in 1984 when they saw that assimilation in New Zealand schools had not worked well for their own children. It became an early childhood Centre of Innovation and was included in the first round of a New Zealand government programme funded from 2003 to 2009. The story of A'oga Fa'a Samoa is told by A'oga Fa'a Samoa teachers, management and Centre of Innovation focus group (2005) and in Podmore *et al.* (2007).

The early childhood Centre of Innovation programme was introduced in the Introduction. It was designed to facilitate research by teachers, supported by research facilitators, that built on innovative approaches and that would 'result in improved early childhood learning and teaching based on Te Whāriki' (Meade, 2005 p.2; see also Meade, 2006, 2007, 2010). In spite of the success of this programme in which teachers researched their own practice and disseminated their findings to hundreds, possibly thousands, of other teachers, it was cut short in mid 2009 as a result of government budget decisions. Ministry of Education professional development programmes continue for a limited number of early childhood centres (see Chapter 8), rather than universal provision for the entire sector and a commentary is included here from Vise, in another Samoan centre, as Figure 1.1. Vise is commenting about her teaching after a professional development programme.

Unifying processes

Helen May comments:

> The latter half of the 1980s was a time of governmental and economic reform: by the 1990s the effects were rippling through all aspects of life in New Zealand . . . Labour [the Labour Government from 1984 to 1990] was persuaded that there was a crisis in early childhood, and that an increased investment would bring benefits to children, women, families, communities and the nation. Early childhood education moved to centre stage on the government's agenda. The

Vise from Samoa Taumafai Aoga Amata

"I see the clear picture of who I am as a teacher and the learning that's inside that drives me to be determined to be able to get deep into the children's learning and to find out more about each child . . . It makes me think that each child has their own unique way of learning, and for us to foster that learning, the child will grow up to become a competent learner and the same with their interests . . . that's something that I'm passionate about with the children . . . coming into a loving environment and to know that when their parents walk in, the children are learning a lot during the day . . . and taking their portfolios home which is marvellous for me as a teacher to see parents asking for their portfolios. And having parents' night, it's quite a good turn out now. And sitting with them and talking about the children's learning, it's so exciting to hear them saying to their children, you've gone a long way and now look at it. And those parents love to write down their voice . . ."

Figure 1.1 Vise from Samoa Taumafai Aoga Amata

subsequent reforms were part of the wider educational and governmental restructuring but, more particularly, the result of orchestrated campaigns by early childhood groups (May, 2009 p.204).

The 1980s and 1990s saw five dramatic unifying processes coordinating the diversity of services and philosophies and having a direct bearing on the integrated approach to curriculum. These were:

- the shift to a common administration;
- integrated teacher education;
- inclusive forums that influence policy;
- coordinated government reviews;
- and a combined teacher union with a strong voice.

The shift to a common administration.   In 1986 all early childhood services except kōhanga reo were brought together under the administration of the Department of Education, replacing the previous system where childcare was under the administration of the Department of Social Welfare and kindergartens and playcentres were administered by the Department of Education. Kōhanga reo were moved to the Department of Education in 1990. These changes made New Zealand a world leader in integrating care and education provision in education. According to the Organization for Economic Cooperation and Development (OECD, 2001, 2006, 2011), countries with strong early childhood education and care systems have developed a systematic and integrated approach to policy, centering predominantly on children as a social group with rights, such as those expressed in the aspirations statement in Te Whāriki (noted early in this chapter). This integration and focus enabled decisions to be made in the interests of children from a united rather than fragmented perspective, and education to be foregrounded.

Integrated teacher education.   In 1988, 3-year integrated early childhood teacher education in colleges of education replaced a divided system of 2-year training for kindergarten teachers and 1-year training for child-care workers. The previous divided approach implied that childcare was a welfare and predominantly 'care' service for disadvantaged children, while kindergartens were educational (Dalli, 1992; May Cook, 1985; May, 1992). New teacher education programmes were required to 'be inclusive of care and education, cover programmes for the care of babies and have more emphasis on education studies and the cultural and family contexts of children's lives' (May, 2009, p.207).

Inclusive forums that influence policy.   Department of Education Lopdell courses (at a venue called Lopdell House) were held to provide think tank forums for policy formulation. These involved key people across all the early childhood groups and have been crucial in the development of a cohesive approach to the early childhood curriculum among diverse organisations and services. Most important was the 1988 Lopdell Curriculum Statement, which identified 15 basic principles of early child-

Table 1.1 Fifteen basic principles of early childhood, 1988

The curriculum will enable all children to experience an environment in which:

they learn who they are	they learn in appropriate ways	decision-making is shared
they are safe	they respect the natural environment	conflict is resolved peacefully
they are healthy	there are goals for children	the importance of home and family is recognised
they relate positively to each other	learning is not limited by gender	adults are learners
they enjoy themselves	learning is not limited by race or colour	people are accountable

hood curriculum (Table 1.1) (New Zealand Department of Education, 1998). The same statement defined the curriculum as 'the sum total of the child's direct and indirect learning experiences', a forerunner to the definition in Te Whāriki (p.10): 'The term *curriculum* is used in this document to describe the sum total of the experiences, activities, and events, whether direct or indirect, which occur in an environment designed to foster children's learning and development'.

Coordinated government reviews. A major review of early childhood education occurred in 1988, alongside reviews of schooling and tertiary education. The government formed a working group chaired by Dr Anne Meade that aimed to establish 'a more equitable system of early childhood care and education' (Early Childhood Care and Education Working Group, 1988, Foreword). This was published as the Meade Report, *Education to be More*. The working group was required to take into account five underlying themes identified by a 1987 Royal Commission on Social Policy that underpin all areas of social policy reform in New Zealand (Early Childhood Care and Education Working Group, 1988, p.v):

- implementing the principles of the Treaty of Waitangi;
- improving the social and economic status of women;
- providing a legislative environment which safeguards basic human rights and freedoms and works towards the removal of discrimination;
- recognising the needs, contributions and traditions of Pacific Island peoples and other minority cultures residing in New Zealand;
- enhancing the family unit in New Zealand society.

A government policy document *Before Five* (Lange, 1988) followed, setting out the early childhood policy, building on *Education to be More* and
promising equal status with other education sectors. National guidelines and charters were to provide overall standards for all early childhood services, and qualification requirements and funding were to be
reviewed. A number of working parties with broad community repre-
sentation were established to implement *Before Five*. The Working Party
on National Guidelines, Charters and Minimum Standards was set up to
define the government's role in the early childhood curriculum. It was
chaired by Helen May, who later became, with Margaret Carr, one of the
writers of Te Whāriki. One upshot of the working party report and policy
implementation was that management was required to provide a programme rationale for the programme, and involve parents and staff in
discussions on it. The programme was required to be developmentally
appropriate for children with special needs, and provide 'for children to
become and remain confident in their own culture and the culture of
Aotearoa New Zealand'.

A combined teacher union with a strong voice. Finally, in 1990 the two early
childhood unions, the Kindergarten Teachers Association and Early
Childhood Workers Union, amalgamated. Underlying the amalgamation
was the desire to form a strong united voice for practitioners in early
childhood education and influence policy and equitable employment
conditions. Later, in 1993 this union joined a powerful union for teachers
and support staff in the primary school sector.

In 1991 the government revised the school curriculum to include
achievement objectives for different age groups for each subject level. It
then turned its attention towards an early childhood curriculum. The
stage was now set for the development of Te Whāriki.

Key points

1. Te Whāriki is a national early childhood curriculum that includes
    children from the ages of 0–4. Children usually go to school on their
    fifth birthday.
2. In order to understand and implement principles from Te Whāriki,
    the following key aspects must be considered:

    i. the contextual, cultural and historical features underpinning its development;

    ii. the principles, pedagogies and early childhood practices following on from its development and

    iii. the ways in which some of those principles, pedagogies and early childhood practices might be useful for early childhood practice elsewhere.

3. The Aotearoa New Zealand story might be described as cultural and governmental settlements, and durable historical, social and cultural commitments to particular forms of education and, indeed, forms of life. The Treaty of Waitangi is an important document, guiding policy.

4. Aotearoa New Zealand was called the social laboratory of the world for its welfare state policies.

5. The nation's values are reflected in Te Whāriki's focus on equity and respect for children's rights as well as its aim to support children in a growing democracy.

6. A diversity of ECCE provision preceded the development of Te Whāriki. This influenced the development of the curriculum.

7. The development of kōhanga reo and playcentres were unique to the history of early childhood in Aotearoa New Zealand.

8. A number of unifying processes preceded and influenced the development of the curriculum:

    i. kindergartens and childcare provision came under the same ministry

    ii. teacher education for all teacher-led services was integrated

    iii. inclusive forums influenced policy

    iv. reports and working parties set the scene

    v. the early childhood unions combined together.

Reflective questions

- Can you share your understanding of the histories of early childhood in your country?
- Whose voices have told these stories? Where can you find them?
- How, do you think, have these histories influenced some key features of early childhood provision now?
- What are the key features of the history of the early childhood setting that you know best? How, do you think, have the histories' cultural

and governmental settlements influenced some key features of the early childhood provision in this centre now?

■ In this chapter, Allan Luke was quoted as saying the following about the education and curriculum stories of Singapore, Finland and Ontario. He says that they

> are not about the triumph of scientific methods. They are not about the triumph of markets, or successful standardization. They are about cultural and governmental settlements, about durable historical, social, and cultural commitments to particular forms of education and, indeed, forms of life (Luke, 2011 p.374).

What does this quote mean? Can you make links with these ideas and your ideal education system?

■ How would you define the innovation in an early childhood centre that you know well?

■ What would be your *aspirations statement* for an early childhood curriculum?

■ Read the comments from Vise in Figure 1.1. Think about and share any new insights you might have developed about being a teacher and teaching, and where these new ideas came from.

Notes

1. As will become apparent in this book, Te Whāriki is a bicultural and bilingual document, and we follow a familiar practice of frequently referring to the country as Aotearoa New Zealand. Aotearoa is the Māori name; it refers to the Long White Cloud that covered the North Island as the first Māori settlers approached. We use a number of Māori words in this book; a glossary at the end explains their meaning.

2. A Māori language claim put before a Waitangi Tribunal in 1985 asserted that te reo Māori (the Māori language) was a taonga that needed to be nurtured. The tribunal released its recommendations in 1986. It recommended several ways for the government to remedy breaches of the Treaty regarding te reo. Brenda adds: 'so I would say that in the eyes of the Māori nation, when the Treaty refers to 'taonga', we consider te reo Māori to be a taonga'.

References

A'oga Fa'a Samoa teachers, management, and Centre of Innovation Focus Group (2005) Innovation at A'oga Fa'a Samoa. In A. Meade (ed.) *Catching the Waves: Innovation in Early Childhood Education*. Wellington: NZCER Press.

Dalli, C. (1992) Policy agendas for children's lives. *New Zealand Journal of Educational Studies*, 27(1), 53–67.

Davey, J. (1998) *Tracking Social Change in New Zealand*. Wellington: Institute of Policy Studies, Victoria University of Wellington.

Early Childhood Care and Education Working Group (1988) *Education to Be More*. Wellington: Government Print.

Government Review Team (1988) *Government Review of Te Kōhanga Reo: Language Is the Life Force of the People*. Wellington: Te Kōhanga Reo National Trust.

Hill, D., Reid, R. and Stover, S. (2000) More than educating children: the evolutionary nature of Playcentre's philosophy of education. In S. Stover (ed.), *Good Clean Fun: New Zealand's Playcentre Movement* (pp.30–8). Wellington: New Zealand Playcentre Federation.

King, M. (2003) *The Penguin History of New Zealand*. Auckland: Penguin Books.

Lange, D. (1988) *Before Five*. Wellington: Government Print

Luke, A. (2011) Generalizing across borders: policy and the limits of educational science. *Educational Researcher*, 40(8), 367–77.

May Cook, H. (1985) *Mind that Child*. Wellington: Blackberry Press.

May, H. (1992) After 'Before Five': The politics of early childhood care and education in the nineties. *New Zealand Women's Studies Journal*, 8(2), 83–100.

May, H. (1997) *The Discovery of Early Childhood*. Wellington: NZCER with Auckland University Press and Bridget Williams Books.

May, H. (2009) *Politics in the Playground. The World of Early Childhood Education in New Zealand* (2nd edn). Dunedin: Otago University Press.

May, H. (2011) *I Am Five and I Go to School. Early Years Schooling in New Zealand, 1900–2010*. Dunedin: Otago University Press.

Meade, A. (ed.) (2005) *Catching the Waves: Innovation in Early Childhood Education*. Wellington: NZCER Press.

Meade, A. (ed.) (2006) *Riding the Waves: Innovation in Early Childhood Education*. Wellington: NZCER Press.

Meade, A. (ed.) (2007) *Cresting the Waves: Innovation in Early Childhood Education*. Wellington: NZCER Press.

Meade, A. (ed.) (2010) *Dispersing the Waves: Innovation in Early Childhood Education*. Wellington: NZCER Press.

Mitchell, L., Royal Tangaere, A., Mara, D. and Wylie, C. (2006) Quality in parent/whanau-led services. Retrieved from http://www.educationcounts.govt.nz/publications/ece/36086/36087.

Moss, P. (2009) There are alternatives! Markets and democratic experimentalism in early childhood education and care. Working Paper No. 53. The Hague: Bernard van Leer Foundation and Bertelsmann Stiftung.

Moss, P. and Petrie, P. (2002) *From Children's Services to Children's Spaces*. London: RoutledgeFalmer.

New Zealand Department of Education (1988) The curriculum: an early childhood statement, Lopdell report. Wellington: New Zealand Department of Education.

Organization for Economic Cooperation and Development (OECD) (2001) *Starting Strong: Early Childhood Education and Care*. Paris: OECD.

OECD (2006) *Starting Strong II: Early Childhood Education and Care*. Paris: OECD.

OECD (2011) *Starting Strong III: A Quality Tool Box for Early Childhood Education and Care*. Paris: OECD.

Podmore, V. N., Wendt Samu, T., Taouma, J. and Tapusoa, E. (2007) Ua mae' a le galuega/Journey's End: key findings from the Aoga Fa'a Samoa. In A. Meade (ed.) *Cresting the Waves: Innovation in Early Childhood Education* (pp.11–18). Wellington: NZCER Press.

Reedy, T. (2003) Toku rangatiratanga na te mana-matauranga. 'Knowledge and power set me free . . .' In J. Nuttall (ed.), *Weaving Te Whāriki: Aotearoa New Zealand's Early Childhood Curriculum Document in Theory and Practice* (pp.51–77). Wellington: NZCER Press.

Sahlberg, P. (2010) *Finnish Lessons: What Can the World Learn from Educational Change in Finland*. New York: Teachers College Press.

Somerset, G. (1976a) *I Play and I Grow: Playcentres in New Zealand*. Auckland: New Zealand Playcentre Federation.

Somerset, G. (1976b) *Vital Play in Early Childhood*. Auckland: New Zealand Playcentre Federation.

Tobin, J. J., Hsueh, Y. and Karasawa, M. (2009) *Preschool in Three Cultures Revisited*. Chicago: University of Chicago Press.

United Nations (1989) *United Nations Convention on the Rights of the Child*. Geneva: UN.

United Nations Committee on the Rights of the Child (1997) Concluding observations of the committee on New Zealand. Geneva: UN.

2 The development of Te Whāriki

From Germany, Sibylle Haas writes:

In Germany we learned about Te Whāriki while exploring the assessment model of learning stories. Through the principles of Te Whāriki I began to understand more clearly the link between strengthening our view of children's competencies through understanding and knowing their families. Being exposed to the bicultural content of Te Whāriki and understanding how bicultural practice supports and encourages the participation of families in the education system excites me. I see the possibilities for us here in Germany through links to our own curriculum in the areas of research, communication and wellbeing to investigate further the opportunities to experience and value our own cultural diversity in positive and affirming ways. These are enriching thoughts and concepts to me that have the potential to enable us to move beyond our present situation of valuing and acknowledging cultural diversity to living and accepting the knowledge and wisdom that comes through the cultural diversity and participation of our families and communities.

By the early 1990s early childhood organisations in Aotearoa New Zealand 'saw it was timely to define the curriculum in more detail to both protect and promote the early childhood philosophy' (Carr and May, 1993a, p.47). From the outset, the writers argued for a bicultural approach to curriculum development and content and for diverse services to be able to negotiate their own curriculum. An account of the early development of Te Whāriki and of how the document was written is given by Sarah Te One (2003). She comments (pp.25–26):

The Request for Proposal (Ministry of Education, 1990) called for tenders from potential contractors 'to develop curriculum guidelines for developmentally appropriate programmes for early childhood education' (p.4) . . . Helen May, then Senior Lecturer and Chair of the Department of Early Childhood at the University of Waikato, had signalled her intention to spearhead a proposal from the Waikato region, and received support from the sector to do so (Wells, 1990). When May and Margaret Carr drew up a process for the contract proposal, it represented a re-conceptualisation of the curriculum process, previously dominated by Western models (May, personal communication). This new model treated content, process, context, and evaluation as interdependent features, an idea that could be traced back to the Basic Principles for an Early Childhood Curriculum developed at Lopdell House (New Zealand Department of Education, 1988).

In the curriculum development process the partnership formed with Te Kōhanga Reo National Trust (the overall umbrella organisation for Māori immersion kōhanga reo) was of vital importance. Tilly Reedy and Tamati Reedy were appointed as the two Māori lead writers and were responsible for writing the Māori immersion curriculum for ngā kōhanga reo. They met often with Helen May and Margaret Carr to discuss how to weave the Māori and Pākehā concepts together (Te One, 2003, p.29). In an interview with Sarah Te One, Helen May recalled:

> Tamati and Tilly Reedy presented the Project with a Māori curriculum framework based on the principle of empowerment. I can remember Tamati Reedy spent a day explaining . . . the concepts and their origins in Te Ao Māori [the Māori world]. It was a complete framework and included the five 'wero' – aims for children. Margaret and I then worked with this framework to position the parallel domains for Pākehā . . . These were not translations. (May, personal communication, cited in Te One, 2003, p.33)

Dialogue and negotiation during curriculum development and early implementation

A collaborative and consultative approach to curriculum development was crucial to the widespread support engendered for the curriculum document. Carr and May (2000) have argued they needed to negotiate between three voices:

- government interests in an efficient and competitive economy;
- early childhood practitioners and families from a diversity of services;

- cultural perspectives, national and international early childhood voices 'advocating for equitable educational opportunities and quality early childhood policies and practices' (p.53).

The curriculum development process was organised to ensure dialogue with all parties having an interest in early childhood education. Representatives from all national early childhood organisations, government agencies, universities and research and teacher training institutions sat on an advisory panel and gave feedback on all the papers. A review group was established by the Ministry of Education to represent the government and evaluate the document (Carr and May, 1993c). A curriculum development team of 15 practitioners, trainers and nationally recognised individuals formed the core working group. The curriculum was structured to enable the development of common principles, aims and goals, and also to provide the opportunity to negotiate the identity of diverse provision within the curriculum framework. Six specialist working groups were developed (see Table 2.1), enabling six core 'communities' to have a voice at the curriculum table.

From 1991 to 1993, the framework was developed during a process of circulating a series of working papers and gaining feedback from early childhood educators, from a diversity of services, in local workshops and conference presentations across the country. Draft guidelines were published in 1993 (New Zealand Ministry of Education, 1993), inviting further published feedback (Murrow, 1995). It was through this process of intensive consultation that consensus concerning the proposed curriculum principles and the aims and goals for children was able to be reached amongst the diverse early childhood services (Carr and May, 1993b). The final curriculum was published in 1996 (New Zealand Ministry of Education, 1996; from here on, in this book, referred to as Te Whāriki).

Table 2.1 Specialist working groups in the curriculum development team*

Infant and Toddler Working Group
Young Child Working Group
Māori Immersion Groups (Kōhanga Reo)
Pacific Island Language Groups (Tagata Pasafika)
Home-based Services
Children with Special Needs

* (New Zealand Ministry of Education, 1993, p.157)

Theoretical underpinnings

This collaborative and open-ended approach to the development of the curriculum was reflected in the title of the curriculum. Te Whāriki, introduced to the project by Tamati Reedy, was 'a central metaphor'. In Māori, Te Whāriki is a woven floor mat. It is translated in the document as follows:

> The early childhood curriculum has been envisaged as a whāriki, or mat, woven from the principles, strands, and goals defined in this document. The whāriki concept recognises the diversity of early childhood education in New Zealand. Different programmes, philosophies, structures, and environments will contribute to the distinctive patterns of the whāriki (New Zealand Ministry of Education, 1996, p.11).

Four principles provide the central ideas of the Te Whāriki approach (see the framework at the end of this chapter). Chapters 4, 5, 6 and 7 each discuss one of these principles; together they describe a sociocultural view of learning as empowering, relational, interconnected and holistic.

In an unusual addition for a national curriculum document, an ecological theoretical position is explicitly stated with an entire page on Urie Bronfenbrenner's ecology of human development (Bronfenbrenner, 1979), acknowledging that a child's learning environment 'extends far beyond the immediate setting of the home or early childhood programmes beyond the home' (New Zealand Ministry of Education, 1996, p.19). This describes Bronfenbrenner's depiction of the child's early learning environment as a nested arrangement of structures, like a set of Russian dolls with the individual (in this case, the child or the child and the family) in the centre. These structures are referred to as the microsystem, meso-system, exo-system and macro-system. The microsystem, the first outer layer, is defined by Bronfenbrenner (1979, p.22; italics in the original) as follows:

> A microsystem is a pattern of activities, roles, and interpersonal relations experienced by the developing person in a given setting with particular physical and material characteristics. A *setting* is a place where people can readily engage in face-to-face interaction – home, day care center, playground, and so on. The factors of *activity*, *role*, and *interpersonal relation* constitute the elements, or building blocks, of the microsystem. A critical term in the definition of the microsystem is *experienced*. The term is used to indicate that the scientifically relevant

features of any environment include not only its objective properties but also the way in which these properties are perceived by the person in that environment.

Bronfenbrenner notes that a role is 'a set of behaviors and expectations associated with a position in society, such as that of mother, baby, teacher, friend and so on' (p.25). Included in this chapter as Figure 2.1 is an example of a wordless act of friendship in an early childhood centre. It is

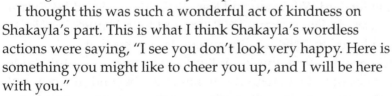

The kindness of a friend

I watched a lovely interaction this afternoon. Kobe was sitting by himself on the step, I think he was feeling very tired, because later he actually fell asleep on the mat. Shakayla noticed Kobe too and without a word she went and got a tractor, put it on his lap, and quietly sat down beside him.

Kobe didn't really respond much at first then he picked the tractor up and had a look at it.

Shakalya sat there quietly, offering unconditional love by her presence.

I thought this was such a wonderful act of kindness on Shakayla's part. This is what I think Shakayla's wordless actions were saying, "I see you don't look very happy. Here is something you might like to cheer you up, and I will be here with you."

A good friend is a great thing and little acts of aroha mean a lot.

Figure 2.1 The kindness of a friend

Written by Julie

these actions that build up expectations about interpersonal relationships: in this case, being and having a friend.

Subsequent levels of ecological structure also influence the child's well-being and capacity to learn. The next level (the mesosystem) consists of the interrelations among two or more settings in which the developing person actively participates (the relationships between the early childhood centre and the home and the local school, for instance). Bronfenbrenner emphasises 'the extent and nature of knowledge and attitudes existing in one setting about the other'. A further level is those settings that do not involve the developing person as an active participant, but in which events occur that affect the developing person. In the case of the young child, this might include a parent's place of work, a school class attended by an older brother or sister, the parents' network of friends, and so on. The outer system includes the nation's beliefs about all these levels and their relationships: the value of ECCE and the rights of children, for instance. Bronfenbrenner reminds us (1979, p.27) that development never takes place in a vacuum; it is always embedded in particular contexts.

The wider economic, social and political policies and actions are central players in the welfare of a nation and its children and families. For many cultural communities there is a wider, all encompassing level: a spiritual domain, defined in a range of ways (Pere, 1988; New Zealand Ministry of Education, 2009; Rameka, 2011). See Rea's story in Chapter 6 for an example of this.

This ecological emphasis is also a reminder to policy-makers and governments that the adults' environment is influential: poverty and inequality of opportunity in the wider society influence the educational achievements of non-dominant groups (those who have little power) in the population. Analysis of data since Te Whāriki was published (for example Richard Wilkinson and Kate Pickett's *The Spirit Level: Why More Equal Societies Almost Always Do Better*, and John Hattie's *Visible Learning*, both published in 2009) has illustrated this connection.

Teachers who find the Te Whāriki approach a useful model will therefore want to look, with Bronfenbrenner, beyond the local setting to the wider context of family, culture and society, to ask 'How do we connect with the other contexts in the children's lives?' Of course, the New Zealand setting is changing too, as globalised market economies and political pressures reduce a government's inclination to vigorously support two key directions for education that enabled the development of Te Whāriki: seizing the opportunity to make up our own collective minds in innovative and culturally relevant ways, and retaining the vision of a democratic and equitable society.

Te Whāriki can be described as taking a sociocultural position on learning and development. This is reflected in Bronfenbrenner's ecological assumptions and the four principles that emphasise empowerment (the aspiration for children and families to have some authority or authorship in their lives), relationships (learning is definited in terms of responsive and reciprocal relationships), family and community (the wider world of family and community is seen as an integral part of the curriculum) and holistic frames (for defining education, beyond traditional categories, for instance, of physical cognitive social and emotional skills). In these principles the definition of education as being about relationships and participation rejected a stage or levelled view of development. However, in an elaboration of each of the goals, three age groups (infants, toddlers and 'young children') provide, in particular, reminders of environments for the especially vulnerable under-twos. This has anticipated a more recent rapid growth in demand for ECE provision for infants and toddlers (Dalli and White, 2011) reflecting in part the woefully poor parental leave provision in Aotearoa New Zealand (one of the lowest in the OECD countries). Mixed age provision is common and the setting out in Te Whāriki of three age groups is controversial – an apparently developmental frame that clashes with the fundamentally sociocultural approach.

The framework

The framework for Te Whāriki included in this chapter is shown in Table 2.2. It begins with the four *curriculum principles* and the *aspirations for children* statement, introduced in this and the previous chapter. The aspirations statement is elaborated in detail as five *strands* of learning outcome: in English, these are belonging, well-being, exploration, communication and contribution. In the document, but not here (there are 117 of them), the strands are further elaborated as 'indicative' (not prescribed) learning outcomes. A number of these indicative outcomes are included in Chapters 4 to 7. In between the principles and the outcomes for children are the features of a facilitating learning environment, the *goals*.

Readers will recognise synergies between Te Whāriki's aspiration statement, principles and strands of outcome and other early childhood curriculum documents developed in the twenty-first century. The title of the first national curriculum for Australia, the 2007 early years' learning

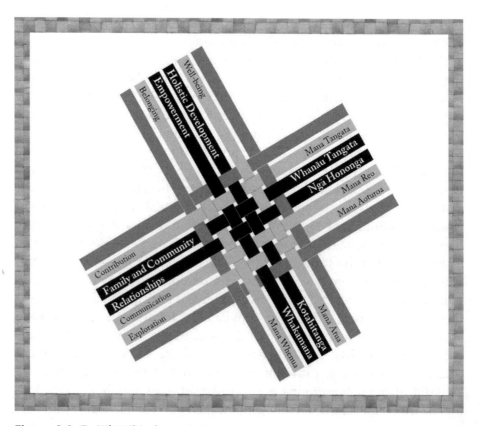

Figure 2.2 Te Whāriki: the weaving

framework, 'Belonging, being and becoming' (Australian Government Department of Education, Employment and Workplace, 2007), signifies an interest in early childhood in its widest sense as a space where learner identities are constructed and diversity is respected. Its five broad learning outcomes are:

- children have a strong sense of identity;
- children are connected with and contribute to their world;
- children have a strong sense of well-being;
- children are confident and involved learners;
- children are effective communicators.

'Pre-birth to three' for Scotland (Learning and Teaching Scotland, 2010) include four key principles for best starts and positive outcomes:

- rights of the child;
- relationships;

Table 2.2 The framework in Te Whāriki

Four principles
An aspirations statement
Five strands
Eighteen goals
117 Indicative outcomes

Relationships – Ngā hononga	Holistic development – Kotahitanga	Family and community – Whānau tangata	Empowerment – Whakamana
Children learn through responsive and reciprocal relationships	The early childhood curriculum reflects the holistic way children learn and grow	The wider world of family and community is an integral part of the early childhood curriculum	The early childhood curriculum empowers the child to grow and learn

Aspirations statement

This curriculum is founded on the following aspirations for children:

to grow up as competent and confident learners and communicators, healthy in mind, body and spirit, secure in their sense of belonging and in the knowledge that they make a valued contribution to society (Te Whāriki p.9)

Well-being – Mana atua	Belonging – Mana whenua	Contribution – Mana tangata	Communication – Mana reo	Exploration – Mana aotūroa
Children will experience an environment where: Goal 1: their health is promoted (4 outcomes)	Children and their families will experience an environment where: Goal 1: connecting links with the family and the wider world	Children will experience an environment where Goal 1: there are equitable opportunities for learning, irrespective	Children will experience an environment where Goal 1: they develop non-verbal communication skills	Children will experience an environment where Goal 1: their play is valued as meaningful learning and the importance of spontaneous play is

Table 2.2 Continued

Well-being – Mana atua	Belonging – Mana whenua	Contribution – Mana tangata	Communication – Mana reo	Exploration – Mana aotūroa
Goal 2: their emotional well-being is nurtured (7 outcomes) Goal 3: they are kept safe from harm (7 outcomes)	are affirmed and extended (6 outcomes) Goal 2: they know they have a place (5 outcomes) Goal 3: they feel comfortable with routines, customs and regular events (5 outcomes) Goal 4: they know the limits and boundaries of acceptable behaviour (6 outcomes)	of gender, ability, age, ethnicity, or background (8 outcomes) Goal 2: they are affirmed as individuals (5 outcomes) Goal 3: they are encouraged to learn with and alongside others (7 outcomes)	for a range of purposes (5 outcomes) Goal 2: they develop verbal communication skills for a range of purposes (8 outcomes) Goal 3: they experience the stories and symbols of their own and other cultures (9 outcomes) Goal 4: they discover and develop different ways to be creative and expressive (9 outcomes)	recognised (6 outcomes) Goal 2: they gain confidence in and control of their bodies (4 outcomes) Goal 3: they learn strategies for active exploration, thinking, and reasoning (5 outcomes) Goal 4: they develop working theories for making sense of the natural, social, physical, and material world (11 outcomes)

- responsive care;
- respect.

(Learning and Teaching Scotland, 2010). The areas of learning in the British Columbia early learning framework (British Columbia Ministry of Health and Ministry of Children and Family Development, 2008) are:

- well-being and belonging;
- exploration and creativity;
- languages and literacies;
- social responsibility and diversity.

The four themes of learning and development in Ireland's 2009 early childhood curriculum framework (National Council for Curriculum and Assessment, 2009) are:

- well-being;
- identity and belonging;
- communicating;
- exploring and thinking.

Early childhood educators will refer to their own official espoused or enacted curricula and policies, comparing these with Te Whāriki in order to provoke discussion and to articulate their own position on the principles and outcomes that matter in the early years.

Key points

1. Dialogue and negotiation characterised the processes of curriculum development and early implementation of Te Whāriki.
2. The collaborative and open-ended approach to the development of the curriculum is reflected in the title of the curriculum, Te Whāriki, translated as a woven mat for all to stand on.
3. The principles, strands and goals provide the framework which allows for different programme perspectives to be woven into the fabric.
4. Te Whāriki is not a curriculum that prescribes aims and content in detail; it expects ECCE services to create their curriculum in a culturally and locally situated way.

5. Te Whāriki describes a sociocultural view of education, and assumes that education and learning will be empowering, holistic, ecological and relational.
6. The curriculum document emphasises an ecological position; this is unusual for a national curriculum document.
7. Te Whāriki has attracted international interest.

Reflective questions

Origins and influences

- What do you know about the history of your country in relation to its curriculum?
- Consider the notion of vertical and horizontal dimensions of expertise and development (see p.66 of this book). Readers should access the Te Whāriki document itself to explore further some of the ideas in this book. The link to Te Whāriki on the Ministry of Education website is http://www.educate.ece.govt.nz/learning/curriculumAndLearning/TeWhariki.aspx.
- Which theorists influenced the development of your curriculum?
- Which theorists have influenced your practice and beliefs most?

Vision and values

- What are the values that shape your practice?
- How do you negotiate values and practices within your early childhood community?

Weaving a curriculum

- How might you go about weaving your own curriculum in your setting?
- Who might you involve?
- What support would you need?

Valued outcomes of ECCE

- What are valued outcomes of ECCE?
- Are these values shared by your colleagues, children and parents?

■ Read 'The kindness of a friend' again. Share any other similar stories. What environments encourage kindness and friendship?

References

Australian Government Department of Education, Employment and Workplace (2007) Belonging, being and becoming. Early years learning framework for Australia. Canberra: DEEWR. Retrieved from www.ag.gov.au/cca.

British Columbia Ministry of Health and Ministry of Children and Family Development (2008) Early learning framework. Retrieved from http://www.bced.gov.bc.ca/early_learning/early_learning_framework.htm.

Bronfenbrenner, U. (1979) *The Ecology of Human Development: Experiments by Nature and Design*. Cambridge, MA: Harvard University Press.

Carr, M. and May, H. (1993a) The role of government in early childhood curriculum in Aotearoa – New Zealand. In V. N. Podmore (ed.) *What Is Government's Role in Early Childhood Education? Papers Presented at the 1993 NZCER Invitational Seminar* (pp. 42–50). Wellington: New Zealand Council for Educational Research.

Carr, M. and May, H. (1993b) *Te Whariki Curriculum Papers. Early Childhood Curriculum Project*. Hamilton: Waikato University.

Carr, M. and May, H. (1993c) Te Whariki: national early childhood curriculum guidelines. Paper presented by Helen May at the International Conference Workshop on Preschool Education: A Change towards the Twenty-first Century, Hong Kong and Hainan, March 20–26. In M. Carr and H. May (eds), *Te Whariki Curriculum Papers*. Hamilton: University of Waikato.

Carr, M. and May, H. (2000) Te Whariki: curriculm voices. In H. Penn (ed.), *Early Childhood Services: Theory, Policy and Practice* (pp. 53–73). Buckingham: Open University Press.

Hattie, J. (2009) *Visible Learning: A Synthesis of over 800 Meta-Analyses Relating to Achievement*. London: Routledge.

Learning and Teaching Scotland (2010) Pre-birth to three. Positive outcomes for Scotland's children and families. National guidance. Retrieved from http://www.educationscotland.gov.uk/earlyyears/prebirthtothree/nationalguidance/index.asp.

Murrow, K. (1995) *Early Childhood Workers' Opinion on the Draft Document Te Whariki*. Research section report series no.5. Wellington: Ministry of Education.

National Council for Curriculum and Assessment (2009) *Aistear: The Early Childhood Curriculum Framework*, National Council for Curriculum Assessment. Principles and themes. Dublin. Retrieved from http://www.ncca.biz/Aistear.

New Zealand Ministry of Education (1993) *Te Whāriki: Draft Guidelines for Developmentally Appropriate Programmes in Early Childhood Services*. Wellington: Learning Media.

New Zealand Ministry of Education (1996) *Te Whāriki. He Whāriki Mātauranga mö ngā Mokopuna o Aotearoa: Early Childhood Curriculum*. Wellington: Learning Media.

Pere, Rangimarie Rose (1988) Te wheke: whaia te maramatanga me te aroha. In S. Middleton (ed.), *Women and Education in Aotearoa* (pp.6–19). Wellington: Allen & Unwin, Port Nicholson Press.

Rameka, L. (2011) Being Māori: culturally relevant assessment in early childhood education. *Early Years,* 31(3), 245–56.

Te One, S. (2003) The context for Te Whāriki: contemporary issues of influence. In J. Nuttall (ed.), *Weaving Te Whāriki* (pp.17–49). Wellington: New Zealand Council for Educational Research.

Wilkinson, R. G. and Pickett, K. (2009) *The Spirit Level: Why More Equal Societies Almost Always Do Better.* London: Allen Lane.

3 Cultural identity and language

From the USA, Margie Carter writes:

> Studying the work of our Aotearoa New Zealand colleagues in crafting an early childhood system and their Te Whāriki curriculum has been a source of new insights and inspiration for so many in North America. In the USA we struggle with a disjointed, underfunded, highly commercialized and politicized approach to early childhood education. New Zealand offers us a different vision for desirable outcomes for our children, and for taking up the challenge of honouring Treaty rights of indigenous peoples and creating a mat for culturally and organizationally diverse groups to stand upon and be strengthened together . . . New Zealand's Te Whāriki curriculum, and the thoughtful work and political will mobilized to bring it into being has infused new thinking and a sense of possibilities for all Americans who have studied it. We have carefully watched the provincial governments of our Canadian neighbours draw inspiration from Te Whāriki to create their curriculum guidelines and realized that we, too, could be taking a very different approach to defining goals and desired outcomes for our youngest citizens.

Introduction

The sections in te reo Māori in Te Whāriki are not direct translations of the English. This chapter, written primarily by one of the authors, Brenda, locates that bilingual and bicultural feature of Te Whāriki as an essential component for understanding Te Whāriki. Threaded through the chapter is the implicit question: 'What is the relevance of the Māori dimensions of Te Whāriki for readers who are not Māori?' There are five themes: world-view, history, language, the birth of Te Kōhanga Reo, and the relevance to Māori and non-Māori of the implementation of Te Whāriki in a Māori educational context.

A Māori world-view

The Māori creation story and tribal traditions are key to understanding Māori cultural identity in a contemporary context. Many of the customs and protocols inherent in Māori ways of being and doing have their roots in the Māori creation story and the narratives that follow. Te reo Māori is viewed as integral to that identity because the original stories are genealogical records in Māori that have been handed down orally from generation to generation. It is believed that once they are translated, part or all of the original essence of those stories is lost. Ranginui Walker says: 'The mythological origins of Māori society are laid out in three major myth cycles, beginning with the creation myth of Ranginui, the sky father, and Papatuanuku, the earth mother' (2004, p.11). The Maui stories, which focus on the demi-god Maui, make up the second phase. The third is concerned with Tawhaki, a key character in the legends who modelled human endeavour and also performed superhuman feats in pursuit of excellence and advancement for humankind. The key characters create the multi-deity structure that underpins a Māori world-view.

The basic social unit in Māori society was the whānau, an extended family which included three generations (Walker, 2004, p.63). A whānau was led by the elders: often four or more. Several whānau groups, as they increased, could also form a hapū (sub-tribe) under the leadership of a common relative from whom the whānau members descended. The iwi (tribe) was the next largest social unit, comprised of related hapū who derived their mana (authority, status or rank) from a common ancestor. All these social units, like the whānau, had a group of leaders who worked collaboratively. The leaders were the elders, who were the repositories of knowledge and the wise ones who mentored their children and grandchildren.

The biological parents of a child did not parent alone. Their siblings had equal authority with parents over the child and carried the same responsibility. This was also the case for the elders and it was common practice for the child to be raised by several adults, including the elders. Many Māori families today still maintain this practice where a grandchild is raised by the grandparents, an aunt or uncle. This upbringing encourages interdependence, rather than independence, where children are taught to stay connected to who they are and where they come from and to put others before self. This style of child-rearing is seen as adding value to the children, enabling them to receive the knowledge and skills held by family members other than the biological parents. It is believed that, in time, the benefits will come back to the whānau, hapū and iwi.

Most early Pākehā who came to Aotearoa New Zealand were Christian or held Christian beliefs. Pākehā society was founded on the belief system that revered one god and one truth, not many gods, the implication being that all other world-views were simply untrue. In the form in which it arrived in Aotearoa New Zealand, Christianity was not tolerant of other views and held generally that Māori beliefs were in conflict with Christian beliefs. The church representatives were on a mission, and 'underlying the mission were ethnocentric attitudes of racial and cultural superiority' (Walker, 2004, p.85). Motivated by a desire to ensure that 'the one truth' was revealed to Māori so that they could be saved from hell and damnation, missionaries set about 'saving' Māori.

The history

Early European influences

Abel Tasman is known as the first European to arrive in Aotearoa New Zealand, in 1642. His was a fleeting visit, following a hostile reception. More than 100 years later James Cook arrived, in 1769, with seal-hunters and timber traders following close behind. Nearly 40 years later, whalers landed in droves:

> The 18th Century bore witness to Māori, a . . . tribal indigenous people meeting a Western European capitalist colonising power. It was with these tangata whenua (first people of the land) that the colonising power, in the form of British Crown representatives, negotiated the Treaty of Waitangi (Te Tiriti o Waitangi), the founding document of this nation (Waho, 2006).

By the late 1830s there were approximately 125,000 Māori in New Zealand and about 2,000 settlers. More immigrants were arriving all the time, and so a British emissary was sent to act for the British Crown to negotiate a treaty between the Crown and Māori. On 6 February 1840 the Treaty of

Waitangi (Te Tiriti o Waitangi) was signed at Waitangi in the Bay of Islands by a representative of the British government, William Hobson, several English residents and approximately 45 Māori rangatira (chiefs). Te Tiriti was taken around Aotearoa New Zealand and by the end of 1840 over 500 Māori had signed it. Te Tiriti represented 'an agreement in which Māori gave the Crown rights to govern and to develop British settlement, while the Crown guaranteed Māori full protection of their interests and status, and full citizenship rights' (Waitangi Tribunal, 2012a). The principles of the treaty are referred to by the Waitangi Tribunal as 'the principle of active protection, the tribal right to self-regulation, the right of redress for past breaches, and the duty to consult. The recognition and adherence to these principles ensure the "active protection" of Māori language and culture' (Waitangi Tribunal, 2012b).

Although Māori by far outnumbered these new visitors, as is the story for other indigenous peoples who were colonised in the same way, by 1840 the Māori population had been decimated. This was mainly due to illnesses introduced from Europe. The other reason for the decline was tribal warfare that escalated with the introduction of muskets: when the first missionaries arrived they traded iron tools and muskets with Māori for food.

Te Tiriti o Waitangi and Te Whāriki

According to Walker, 'The Treaty of Waitangi is the legitimate source of constitutional government in New Zealand. It provided the British Crown with a tenuous beachhead on New Zealand soil' (2004, p.98). In the century that followed, the Crown would extend its power through the 'acquisition, control and, ultimately, expropriation of land' (Walker, 2004, p.98). Since signing the treaty the British Crown, through the consecutive governments who have represented it, have repeatedly failed to protect Māori who, under Te Tiriti, were guaranteed all the rights and privileges of British subjects. There are countless events, many well documented, where the historical facts demonstrate serious breaches of the treaty. However, there have also been genuine attempts to recognise treaty rights and to ensure that legislative documents, government policy and practice are consistent with the principles of the treaty and do not contradict them. Te Whāriki, as the first bicultural curriculum statement developed in Aotearoa New Zealand, is the forerunner of such efforts in the education sector.

In early childhood education settings, all children should be given the opportunity to develop their knowledge and understanding of the cultural heritages of both partners to Te Tiriti o Waitangi. The curriculum reflects this partnership in text and structure (Te Whāriki, p.9). Early childhood services are required to uphold Te Whāriki and make certain their learning programmes align with the document. There are examples of how adults might achieve this in relation to the principles of the treaty throughout the document.

While the sentiment in Te Whāriki is clear, implementing the principles so that they translate into sincere, respectful, reciprocal treaty-based relationships between people, places and things that also span the past, present and future is a complex task. Māori language is integral to Māori identity, and cultural identity has been seriously affected by the steep decline of native Māori language speakers as a result of the colonial experience. The regeneration of any endangered language requires enormous effort on the part of those who belong to the language, for it is initially they who must have an interest in keeping their language alive. The Māori language is no different.

Endangered language and cultural identity: the birth of Te Kōhanga Reo (the language nest)

This section, a discussion of the development of Te Kōhanga Reo, is drawn, with permission, from a presentation to the 8th Early Childhood Convention in 2004 by Penny Poutu (2004).

During the 1970s it became apparent that an increasing majority of Māori no longer spoke the Māori language and had little knowledge of Māori values, beliefs, spirituality and culture. Native speakers of the language were generally older than the rest and their numbers were fast decreasing. Most Māori people no longer lived in their rural, tribal communities and were predominately urban dwellers. The gravity of the situation for Māori was highlighted by their increasing over-representation in negative social statistics in all areas, including justice, housing, health, education and employment. Māori youth began to articulate publicly the anger many Māori felt towards wider Pākehā society, especially the government, because of the historical injustices and the total failure to include Māori in running the country. Although these concerns may have been spoken of in public Māori settings such as marae and tribal gatherings, they had never before been articulated through the media and protests in the ways that developed during the 1970s.

Māori elders empathised with the growing anger among their youth and called for Māori and the government to support the revitalisation of the Māori language and culture. They advised the government via the Department of Māori Affairs to assist older native speakers of the language to connect with the generation of grandchildren in order to pass on these taonga – these highly valued and essential elements of our indigenous Māori identity – to the next generation. Thus, 1982 saw the first Te Kōhanga Reo – the language nest. Hundreds of kōhanga reo sprouted up all over the country as a national desire amongst Māori to save and nurture the language was embraced. This saw older Māori, predominantly women, acting as language models and cultural guides for young children aged from birth to 5 years of age. These women were not alone. The development model that guided kōhanga reo was the 'whānau' – the principal social kinship unit in Māori society, the extended family. This Māori concept of organisation was embraced and created a new whānau model, one based not on genealogical and tribal kinship but on the shared vision of saving a language and culture from extinction. The whānau model meant that everyone was part of this development – children, parents, extended family, staff and supporters. It offered a new kinship which, in the urban setting, allowed non-related people to find new support systems. The nature of Māori society, which requires most formal or traditional situations to include both men and women in matters of protocol, meant that although women were often the mainstay in the daily running of kōhanga reo, it was entirely normal for men to be involved in the process.

The Te Kōhanga Reo National Trust was established as a central administration system. The trustees were highly respected individuals from across the nation and from different tribal areas. Kōhanga Reo became a national movement embracing the Māori nation in a united vision of language revitalisation and regeneration. The approach was revitalisation through a total immersion Māori language environment where Māori cultural values, beliefs and practices have supremacy. It would be fair to say that kōhanga reo were not established as early childhood centres; they did not seek to follow early childhood models and theories. In the initial stages of the development, early childhood philosophy and practice was often regarded as 'Pākehā' and a potential threat to the Māori authenticity of the movement. Kōhanga reo were established first and foremost to save the Māori language and culture and not as caring facilities for children. Having large numbers of young children in one place and providing linguistically rich and stimulating learning environments were challenges that the movement was to encounter after the initial euphoria and joy of the movement's inception. Kōhanga Reo is held in high esteem and status; it has a special place in the hearts and minds of the nation's Māori and the early childhood sector in Aotearoa New Zealand. This was the political climate in which Te Kōhanga Reo o Mana Tamariki was established in 1990.

Te Kōhanga Reo o Mana Tamariki, one Māori educational model, is a case study presented in Chapter 6 which focuses on the principle of whakamana, or empowerment.

Implementing Te Whāriki by Māori and non-Māori in Aotearoa New Zealand

New Zealand is the home of Māori language and culture: curriculum in early childhood settings should promote te reo and nga tikanga Māori, making them visible and affirming their value for children from all cultural backgrounds (Te Whāriki, p.42).

In Māori educational settings

Māori parents who opt for Māori educational settings for their children generally do so because they are deeply committed to the revival of the Māori language and culture and they believe that cultural and linguistic competence in Māori and English is vital to their children. Many Māori parents want their children to be competent, confident, bilingual and bicultural. Their decision to opt out of mainstream education is often a direct result of their own negative schooling experiences in the mainstream.

In a non-Māori educational setting

Since its implementation, Te Whāriki has strengthened the potential of a uniquely Aotearoa New Zealand pedagogical approach to learning for young children that is underpinned by a commitment to Te Tiriti o Waitangi and to the notion that the Māori language and culture are to be protected. To achieve this

adults working with children should understand and be willing to discuss bicultural issues, actively seek Māori contributions to decision making, and ensure that Māori children develop a strong sense of self-worth (Te Whāriki, p.40).

When Māori children and their families are able to enjoy an equitable standard of living, good health and educational success as Māori in Aotearoa New Zealand they will be able to make a valued contribution to society. The benefits of the Māori contribution will be enjoyed by all, Māori and non-Māori alike. Te Whāriki declares (p.43)

> The curriculum should include Māori people, places, and artifacts, and oppor-tunities to learn and use the Māori language through social interaction.

In addition (p.55):

> Liaison with local tangata whenua and a respect for papatuanuku should be promoted . . . Adults working in the early childhood setting should recognise the significance of whakapapa, understand and respect the process of working as a whānau, and demonstrate respect for Māori elders . . . The use of the Māori language and creative arts in the programme should be encouraged, and staff should be supported in learning the language and in understanding issues relating to being bilingual (Te Whāriki, pp.54, 64, 73).

From a Māori perspective, all other peoples who arrived after 1840 are also bound by Te Tiriti o Waitangi and therefore the responsibility to protect the Māori language and culture lies with all citizens of Aotearoa New Zealand. However, not all share this view. The widespread inter-pretation in the early childhood sector in Aotearoa New Zealand is that the implementation of these goals is the responsibility of every adult in the sector, Māori and non-Māori alike, whether or not there are children of Māori descent on the centre's roll. In Book 3, *Bicultural Assessment* in the *Kei Tua o te Pae* series (Carr *et al.*, 2004) examples of learning and teaching from a bicultural perspective are given. In Figure 3.1 Desiree has made her authentic self visible in a learning story designed to ensure that all who read it are aware that she values the wider whānau. In particular, she brings into focus Māori viewpoints about reciprocal and responsive relationships with people, places and things.

Te Whāriki is not the only legislative document that clearly defines the responsibility upon adults in educational settings to protect the Māori language and culture. The New Zealand Teachers Council, the regulatory body for all teachers (early childhood, primary and secondary) in Aotearoa New Zealand, also confirms that 'The Treaty of Waitangi extends equal status and rights to Māori and Pākehā. This places a particular responsibility on all teachers in Aotearoa New Zealand to

Wedding on the beach

He aha te mea nui o Te Ao?
He tangata, He tangata, He tangata!
What is the most important thing
in this world?
It is people, It is people, It is people!

Hi Courtney. Isn't this a small world? He tino iti Te Ao. Here we are at Mount Maunganui at a wedding. The groom is my nephew, Russell, or Poss, as we call him in the family. He is your mum's cousin and his wife is Bex the bride.

It was nice to see you and your family there. And it was fun for me to catch up with your nanny and all your aunties and uncles. It has been a long time since I have seen them all.

I took my mokopuna, Layla and Anahera with me to the wedding. And my other moko Nikau came with his mum and dad. Being part of a large family I am sure we will run in to each other again at other functions. In the meantime it is nice being able to spend time with you at Selwyn Kindergarten and to watch you learn and grow my friend.

Whanaungatanga

He purapura i ruia mai i Rangiātea
E kore e ngaro
A seed sown in Rangiātea will never be lost.

Figure 3.1 Wedding on the beach

> We are who we are because of our whānau and our con-
> nections to other whānau. I may not be an aunty but there is a
> connection that goes back to before you were born Courtney.
> I used to see your mum when she was your age. And your
> great nanny and koro, tino ataahua rāua. Nanny Ngahirata
> used to make us laugh so much, her and Koro Neville were
> really funny and he liked to play jokes on everyone!! I think
> maybe your Koro is like that too! My brother, Russell, was
> married to your aunty Faye, or nanny Faye, koro's sister, and
> they have four children, Teresa, Russell-Marc, Krystal and Te
> Rina. It was Russell's wedding we went to.
>
> Courtney it is the mana or identity of the past that gives us
> pride to be who we are today and through manaakitanga and
> aroha we share and support each other. Sometimes in our
> lives we will have pātaitai, testing and challenging times but
> with whakakata/humour, which I know runs in your veins,
> life and learning can be fun.
>
> Courtney you are developing māramatanga here at Selwyn
> Kindergarten, where you are finding ways of thinking things
> through, as you go about your learning. He kōtiro tino
> arahina koe – in doing so you are becoming a confident and
> self reliant leader e hoa – ka pai e kōtiro!

Figure 3.1 Continued

Written by Desiree

promote equitable learning outcomes'. Fully registered teachers have to
meet 12 specified criteria or key indicators. One of those requires that
teachers 'demonstrate commitment to bicultural partnership in Aotearoa
New Zealand – demonstrate respect for the heritages, languages and
cultures of both partners to the Treaty of Waitangi'. Another criterion
stipulates that teachers 'work effectively within the bicultural context of
Aotearoa New Zealand' (NZ Teachers Council, 2009). The criteria for
fully registered teachers are consistent with Te Whāriki. Teacher education programmes throughout the country include this uniquely Aotearoa
New Zealand approach in their courses.

Despite legislation, the meaningful implementation of Te Whāriki in a way that is relevant to Aotearoa New Zealand is fraught with difficulties for teachers who have little or no knowledge of the Māori language and culture, and especially for those who have had very little engagement with Māori in their lives. There is still a belief among many people that any inequality suffered by Māori in the present day is of their own doing because there is equal opportunity for all in Aotearoa New Zealand. Therefore, a special focus on the Māori language and culture is seen as giving the culture special treatment. Joris de Bres, the New Zealand Race Relations Commissioner, says he still has

a sense that there is a lack of generosity in some Pākehā attitudes to Māori and there is a lack of will to see measures taken that will help to remove that disadvantage and there is a lack of understanding of this notion that it is actually fair to deal specifically with people who are suffering unfairness (Hartevelt, 2012, p.A1).

Ongoing protest and debate illustrate the difficulties that Walker says 'are symptomatic of the on-going Māori struggle for equality and the country's fumbling steps towards mature nationhood' (2004, p.400). Te Whāriki has given the early childhood sector the potential to strengthen the nation by assisting all young children to take up their roles and responsibilities under the Treaty of Waitangi. In fact, Te Whāriki has made it normal, even expected, that non-Māori adults will embark on a journey towards deeper relationships with Māori that in turn will bring clarity to their own role as non-Māori in Aotearoa New Zealand.

He purapura i ruia mai i Rangiātea
E kore e ngaro

A seed sown in Rangiātea
Will never be lost

The Māori language section of Te Whāriki commences with this well-known Māori proverb (Te Whāriki, p.31). Rangiātea is the spiritual homeland where the origin of Māori was planted and remains protected. Every Māori descends from a seed planted at Rangiātea and therefore the cultural identity of every Māori is protected. While individuals may grow up alienated from their Māori roots the Māori believe that the essence of their identity is secure and merely requires active engagement with te ao Māori (the Māori world) to activate it. The use of this proverb to introduce the Māori section of Te Whāriki is a reminder in the early childhood context of the role and responsibility of every adult to ensure Māori children are able to actively engage with their language and culture as a way of building their identity. If every Māori child is assisted to do so then all other children and adults, no matter what their ethnicity is, will in turn be enriched with all that comes with the privilege of participating in the dual heritage of Aotearoa New Zealand.

The relevance of Te Whāriki in another context

Readers may assume that understanding Te Whāriki from a Māori educational context has very little or no relevance to their own context. However, we believe good teachers should remain open to other ways of being and doing, and to the role of cultural identity and language in the well-being of young children in all early childhood settings. Many of the quotes from Te Whāriki in the previous section can be re-worded with other cultural identities and languages in mind. Anyone exploring the Te Whāriki approach, however, must first understand the document in the Aotearoa New Zealand context because that is where it has its roots. Loris Malaguzzi, architect of the Reggio Emilia pedagogical approach, when asked by Lella Gandini about the schools of thought that influenced the formulation of the Reggio approach, said:

> We must, however, state right away that we also emerged out of a complex cultural background. We are immersed in history, surrounded by doctrines, politics, economic forces, scientific change, and human dramas; there is always in progress a difficult negotiation for survival (Malaguzzi, 1998, p.58).

There is a similar story behind the genesis of Te Whāriki. In the same way that the caretakers of the world-renowned Reggio approach maintain that their system cannot be duplicated outside its cultural context, Te Whāriki cannot just be picked up and implemented effortlessly beyond the shores of Aotearoa New Zealand. Nevertheless, it is an example of a cross-cultural curriculum, designed with a vision of citizens who value democracy and empowerment, relationships, and a holistic view of children in a culturally aware linguistic, family and community context. Others may take a significant interest in or inspiration from Te Whāriki and, indeed, the principles may be applied successfully elsewhere, but Te Whāriki will always belong to and be most effective in Aotearoa New Zealand.

Key points

1. Cultural world-views are implicit in developing and implementing the curriculum, and recognising this is important for understanding.
2. The history of the local and wider community is relevant to understanding a curriculum.
3. Language is central to cultural identity, and identity is a central feature of an early childhood curriculum approach.
4. Te Whāriki is a bilingual and bicultural document that has developed in a unique historical and cultural context.
5. Māori contexts are relevant to reflexive practice elsewhere.

Reflective questions

■ How is (or might) the culture and language of indigenous peoples in the country you know best be protected, supported and enhanced at each level of Bronfenbrenner's model?
■ What role might you be able to play in this, and at what level?
■ What are some of the rich contexts in which very young children develop language, and develop more than one language?
■ Thinking of your own home language, what evidence of the development of rich and complex language do you value and would you look for? What opportunities in your local early childhood provision would ensure that these features develop and flourish?
■ There is a spiritual dimension to life and learning for many people. What connections might you make to this?
■ What reading about cultural identity and language has influenced you? And, having read it, what difference did it make to your thinking?
■ Read Figure 3.1 (Wedding on the beach) again. 'We are who we are because of our whānau (extended family) and our connections to other whānau'. Discuss what this means to you.

References

Carr, M., Lee, W. and Jones, C. (2004, 2007 and 2009) *Kei Tua O Te Pae. Assessment for Learning: Early Childhood Exemplars*. Books 1–20. A resource prepared for the Ministry of Education. Wellington: Learning Media.

Hartevelt, J. (2012) Commentary. 6 February, Wellington: *The Dominion Post*.

Malaguzzi, L. (1998) History, ideas and basic philosophy. In C. Edwards, L. Gandini and G. Forman (eds), *The Hundred Languages of Children: The Reggio Emilia Approach – Advanced Reflections* (2nd edn) (pp.113–25). Westport, CT: Ablex

New Zealand Ministry of Education (2009) *Te Whatu Pōkeka: Kaupapa Māori Assessment for Learning.* Wellington: Learning Media.

New Zealand Teachers Council (2009) Registered teachers criteria. Retrieved from http://www.teacherscouncil.govt.nz/rtc/rtc.pdf.

Poutu, P. (2004) Mana tamariki. Unpublished presentation to the 8th Early Childhood Convention. Palmerston North, New Zealand.

Waho, T. (2006) Panel discussion. Unpublished presentation at Reggio study tour. Reggio Emilia.

Waitangi Tribunal (2012a) Meaning of the Treaty. Retrieved from http://www.waitangi-tribunal.govt.nz/treaty/principles.asp.

Waitangi Tribunal (2012b) The principles of the Treaty. Retrieved from http://www.waitangi-tribunal.govt.nz/treaty/principles.asp.

Walker, Ranginui (2004) *Ka Whawhai Tonu Matou Struggle Without End.* Auckland: Penguin (1st edn, 1990).

4 Principle one: Ngā honongā/ relationships

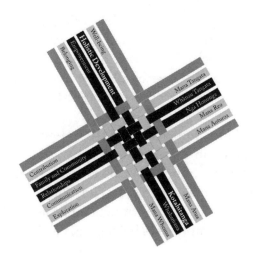

When I think about relationships, a quote from Groundwater-Smith and White comes to mind: 'Schools which actively strive to dignify the lives of all who participate in them, challenging and difficult though the task may be, are indeed contributing to a more moral and just world' (1995, p.197). Developing responsive and reciprocal relationships with a view to dignifying the lives of all who are part of our learning community, supporting wise and happy learners is at the heart of our philosophy. Giving consideration to how we enliven learning where thought is given to a 'moral and just world' is a good challenge for us! Manaakitanga, which we view as kindness, hospitality and respect, is a learning power that is really valued, shared and made visible here (Teacher reflection, Marianne).

This chapter introduces the curriculum principle (ngā honongā/relationships) that describes in a succinct way a key feature of the sociocultural philosophy of teaching and learning in Te Whāriki. In English, this principle is elaborated as 'children learn through responsive and reciprocal relationships with people, places, and things'. One writer who describes a social or relational theory of learning is Jean Lave. Writing in the same year as the publication of Te Whāriki, she says:

> Common theories of learning begin and end with individuals (although these days they often nod at 'the social' or 'the environment' in between). Such theories are deeply concerned with individual differences, with notions of better and worse, more or less learning, and with comparison of these things across groups-of-individuals. Psychological theories of learning prescribe ideals and pathways to excellence and identify the kinds of individuals (by no means all) who should arrive . . . A reconsideration of learning as a social, collective, rather than individual, psychological phenomenon offers the only way beyond the current state of affairs that I can envision at the present time (Lave, 1996, p.149).

In the sociocultural literature, James Wertsch (1998 p.65) has emphasised 'living in the middle', in the relationship between the individual and the collective or the environment. This is more than just a nod at the social or the environmental spheres, and it is this *responsive and reciprocal relationship* that describes the learning emphasis in Te Whāriki. The curriculum document emphasises belonging, participation, community:

> Each community to which a child belongs, whether it is a family home or an early childhood setting outside the home, provides opportunities for new learning to be fostered: for children to reflect on alternative ways of doing things; make connections across time and place; establish different kinds of relationships; and encounter different points of views. These experiences enrich children's lives and provide them with the knowledge skills and dispositions they need to tackle new challenges (Te Whāriki, p.9).

A commentary on learning outcomes adds:

> Dispositions to learn develop when children are immersed in an environment that is characterised by well-being and trust, belonging and purposeful activity, contributing and collaborating, communicating and representing, and exploring and guided participation (Te Whāriki, p.45).

Another teacher reflection emphasises the environment:

> The environment has a huge impact on us as social beings. We have seen that spaces can either bring us together or keep us apart so we work to develop our centre as a 'place to connect' – a place to connect with each other, with new ideas, and with interesting resources that children can use in many different ways. We plan our environment so that it promotes our values of respect and collaboration, and the teachers try to work with children in small groups, where everyone has an opportunity to share ideas, discuss, disagree and debate (Teacher reflection, Jacqui).

Relationships with people

Relationships with people, and relational pedagogy, underly this principle (Peters, 2009). The importance in early childhood programmes of sustained shared thinking with other people has been highlighted by the Effective Provision of Pre-school Education longitudinal study in the UK (Sylva *et al.*, 2010):

> The 'excellent' settings were thus found to encourage 'sustained shared thinking', a concept that came to be defined as any episode in which two or more individuals 'worked together' in an intellectual way to solve a problem, clarify a concept, evaluate activities, extend a narrative, etc. (Sylva *et al.*, 2010, p.157).

Language, language genre and dialogue are of central interest in the educational world. Neil Mercer and Karen Littleton, for instance, write in 2007 about the central role of dialogue in the development of children's thinking, and there are examples in a paper by Margaret (Carr, 2011) about young children reflecting on their learning and teachers' conversation strategies. 'Dialogue' is not always about language, as teachers of young children who are skilled at a pedagogy of noticing, recognising and responding acknowledge (Cowie, 2000; Mason, 2002; see the 'filter' in the Acknowledgements and Introduction). In a research paper written by two teachers from a TLRI action research project (see acknowledgement on p.xi), published in the *Early Childhood Folio*, stories are told of one of these reciprocal relationships as a negotiation between teachers and children during a project entitled 'Stone Crazy' in which teachers and children became mutually engaged with an opportunity for carving. Teachers in this project write:

> Both the intentional teacher and the intentional learner inhabit the same space, a space where teaching and learning roles are interchanged and the direction and the goals are co-constructed (Robinson and Bartlett, 2011, p.11).

After describing the stone-carving project, and two of the children's very different approaches to the opportunity, the teachers conclude:

> The powerful learning space where these intentional teachers and learners met was a site with rich opportunities for co-inquiry, where participants could share the roles of learning and teaching, and connect with a broader 'real-life' community.

In the same issue of this journal a primary school teacher and a research coordinator developed the metaphor of a bivalve mollusc shell (a *tuangi*, or New Zealand clam) in which two shells are connected to each other. This metaphor illustrates the reciprocal relationship between a resourceful teacher and a resourceful learner in an ecological and cultural context in a school with Māori-medium and English-medium classrooms (Simpson and Williams, 2011).

We are still finding greater depths of understanding from these ideas in the research and philosophical thinking and discussions that have followed the publication of Te Whāriki – discussions that often return us to earlier thinkers and writers and the wisdom of the past. As we think about the central role of relationships in teaching and learning in Aotearoa New Zealand we often refer to a waiata composed by Hirini Melbourne (2009) and adopted by the early childhood community:

> *E tu kahikatea*
> *He whakapae ururoa*
> *Awhi mai, awhi atu,*
> *Tatou tatou e*

> Stand like the *kahikatea* [tree],
> stand against the storm,
> together, united, we will survive.

Relationships with place

Place-based education has an extensive literature now (for example, Brian Wattchow and Mike Brown's *A Pedagogy of Place*, 2011, and Doreen

Massey's *For Space*, 2005). Referring to Te Whāriki, Pam Whitty writes the following in a commentary on the development of the New Brunswick Curriculum Framework (NBCF) in Canada:

> There was a moment in the midst of the NBCF project when I wanted to formally name the finished document *A Sense of Place*. I had been thinking of Te Whāriki and the metaphorical meaning of woven mat. I was imagining what metaphor might work for this New Brunswick document. Place plays a critical role in the co-construction of the document; place is specific and yet at the same time it could be metaphorical . . . My childhood nostalgia and my own sense of belonging with/in/to the land of New Brunswick is what brought me back to New Brunswick in the 1970s (Whitty, 2009, pp.51–52. She continues with theorising about place pedagogies as local, storied and contested).

A story of four children going on a bus to visit one of the children's homes (Figure 4.1) offers a many-faceted episode about relationships, in this case with people and place.

Relationship with things

There is much to say about children's (and adults') relationships with *things*. Although the curriculum possibly has primarily in mind children playing with objects in the early childhood setting, adults, too, work and play with objects as 'mediational means'. Museums tell the stories of objects' relationships in communities. A book subtitled '*Object Stories from Te Manawa*', from the collection in a New Zealand museum that has a close relationship with the local kōhanga reo, edited by Fiona McKergow and Kerry Taylor (2011), beautifully illustrates this point. Kate Pahl and Jennifer Rowsell (2010) write about the role of objects in storytelling, symbolising and representing relationships and events that matter (*Artifactual Literacies: Every Object Tells a Story*). Objects in early childhood provision provide props for dramatic play and the taking on of a new identity; blocks, sand tools, books, trees, paintbrushes, computers and pencils enable young children to symbolise, represent, imagine, problem-solve, find out, play and learn.

Material objects cross boundaries, connecting home and early childhood centre: photographs, food, works of art and the stories that are attached to them. Etienne Wenger writes about belonging, one of the strands in the New Zealand early childhood curriculum, emphasising the role of place as well as materials:

Tangata!

This afternoon four great friends headed off on a shared adventure together. It had been talked about for days and now finally the time had come, how excited we were. Myself (Wendy), Lusungu, Daniel, Tanieka and Dulcie headed off on a Wednesday afternoon to catch the bus that would take us all to Lusu's home. Together we sat at the bus stop keenly awaiting the number '59' bus as we chatted about our approaching visit. After a short wait '59' arrived and the almost empty bus delivered us nearly to Lusu's door. Lusungu led us through his gate and opened his home to his friends with his Dad Thomas and sister Towela there to greet us. With a short pause at the door to take shoes off, the posse of friends entered the house as Lusu enthusiastically guided them down the hall to his room. The girls took a detour at his sister's room and went in there with her to explore what she had to play with and to spend time with their new young friend. From Towela's room to Lusu's and then out to the yard our four friends moved, there was a lot to investigate . . . Who was Lusungu when he wasn't at Mitchell Street? What did he like to do? Where would he spend his time when he was at home? Who was his family?

Figure 4.1 Tangata!

Written by Wendy P.

Talking about learning in terms of these modes of belonging makes it possible to consider educational designs not just in terms of the delivery of a curriculum, but more generally in terms of their effects on the formation of identities. Students need:

1. places of engagement
2. materials and experiences with which to build an image of the world and themselves
3. ways of having an effect on the world and making their actions matter (1998, p.270).

A national curriculum document is also one of these materials or things, as are assessment portfolios. And so are carpentry tools, useful for solving problems, as Eden illustrates in the story 'Eden the builder'.

Eden the builder

Eden, you came across the inside barrier connector and found that the nails were not completely in. You went outside and soon came back with a hammer. You studied the nails again and then began to hammer them in. You stopped after a couple of bangs and re-checked the position of the nails. Then you continued.

Wendy's reflection

Eden clearly noticed the poking out nail heads and also worked out a solution to the problem. She has a good understanding of when and how to use the carpentry tools. This really shows that Eden develops a working theory for making sense of the physical world. She is also able to use the technologies around us, that is using tools to solve real problems. Well done, Eden.

Figure 4.2 Eden the builder

Written by Wendy X.

Indicative learning outcomes

In Te Whāriki, the goals, as a description of the facilitating environment, are followed by indicative, rather than definitive, learning outcomes, as Chapter 2 pointed out. The vocabulary is important. Pam Whitty writes about the language of outcomes, a good topic for discussion:

> Because the New Zealand writers textualized outcomes, the designers of the NBCF could think about the language of outcomes and ask questions such as how does this work here in NB, or is there a different choice? What linguistic term (linguistic turn) can we take textually and politically as we engage in this conscious effort to shift more fully into postfoundational theories and practices? How will this shift work for educators, children, families and policy makers? Instead of using the language of outcomes, we decided to go with broad-based learning goals (Whitty, 2009, p.43).

These broad-based learning goals in the NBCF are: well-being, play and playfulness, communication and literacies, and diversity and social responsibility. Pam Whitty quotes Peter Moss on the vocabulary of developmentalism:

> It privileges instrumental rationality and technical practice; its prime question being 'what are the outcomes?' and 'what works?' In doing so, it sets up a binary opposition between process and outcomes (Moss, 2007, p.229).

In Te Whāriki the learning outcomes turn the strand nouns (belonging, well-being etc.) into indicative verbs and actions. Examples of these are 'What does this look like?', 'How will we know it when we see it?' and 'What are we striving for?' As indicative (not prescribed) outcomes their purpose invites and informs local pedagogical discussions. The verbs remind us that the nouns are a construction, a work-in-progress, both process and perhaps outcomes. However, as a curriculum text, 'outcomes' can be dangerous territory when we want to steer away from deficit-based assessment identifiers and emphasise action in context and learning in relationships. There are 117 indicative learning outcomes. Accompanied by narrative assessments (also adopted by New Brunswick teachers), the verbs can keep the context alive and relevant. These aspects of the curriculum are discussed further in Chapter 5, where we discuss the notion in Te Whāriki of outcomes as working theories and learning dispositions. Readers may also like to read a discussion on 'Educational outcomes, modern and postmodern interpretations' by Andy Hargreaves and Shawn Moore (2000), drawing on research in Canada and Australia.

A Case study: Greerton Early Childhood Centre

Background information

Greerton Early Childhood Centre is the first of five Centres of Innovation case studies used in Chapters 4 to 8 to illustrate practice. Greerton is a full day early learning and care centre; children attend from early infancy until they go to school (which in New Zealand is around 5 years old). There are two settings – renovated houses, not purpose-built buildings – one for infants and toddlers, and, a 5-minute walk away, a centre for toddlers and young children.

Set in an area of low- to middle-income housing, most children come from the surrounding area, but a number of children come from all over the city, Tauranga (population 106,000), in the North Island of New Zealand. On any day each setting is attended by around 25 children in the infant and toddler centre and 35 children in the toddler and young children's centre, and all teachers are qualified, with a 3-year degree or diploma in early childhood.

As a framework for their Centre of Innovation project, the teachers describe their centre as having a 'question-asking' and 'question-exploring' culture. This focus reflects their interest in investigating aspects of responsive and reciprocal relationships, a principle that was already evident in their practice.

The following examples of opportunities for responsive and reciprocal relationships between children and between adults and children are taken from their final report.

Mana whenua – belonging. The children plan modifications to the outdoor area and observe the changes unfolding

At the heart of learning and teaching for the teachers at Greerton is their responsibility to build a sense of belonging for children and their families. Throughout their research the teachers kept returning to the concept of belonging, using this as a measure to work out what was involved in building reciprocal, responsive relationships with children, their families and teachers. They realised just how essential listening was in this process. They comment:

> Intuitive, active listening and full attention enable teachers to build relationships with children and their families, allowing learning to flourish from all perspectives. We believe that this underpins teachers' abilities to notice, recognise and respond to children and their learning.

As their research progressed they talked a great deal about what this might mean for infants. Understanding an infant's wishes requires deep listening by teachers who know them very well. It also entails giving them freedom, space and time to explore, as active learners involved and engaged in making decisions about their learning. Right from the very beginning, building a sense of belonging was connected to a listening dialogue. It was also very important to find that space between teachers' intentions and children's intentions in order to build a collaborative learning setting.

Mana atua – well-being. A valuing-in-action of playfulness and joy

The teachers comment that playfulness can be seen in the delight of shared laughter between friends who know each other well and who have a shared repertoire of events of 'silliness' and mischief. Many of these events are engineered by the teachers. On one occasion 4-year-old Cam hid in a large cardboard box and Robert (a teacher) and some children wrote a label addressing this as a parcel for Melissa (another teacher). The children ran to tell Melissa that there was a parcel for her, and the unsuspecting teacher was suitably astonished when her 'parcel' began to wriggle, to the hilarity of all.

They value joy at Greerton, too, and a wonderful photograph illustrates the joy on a baby's face as one of the teachers gently shakes a cherry blossom tree and a cascade of white blossoms fall in front of her.

Mana aotūroa – exploration. Replacing routine with rhythm, seeking children's implicit questions

The teachers at Greerton replaced routine with rhythm in order not to interrupt focused play, so that 'things that really matter had the time, the space and the value granted to them to enable children to become deeply involved in exploring the world around them'. Play is not time-managed and schedule-framed (Final report, p.19):

> Flynn takes such a long time to explore what is going on around him and is often the last child to arrive at lunch-time in the mornings. This is a time when there are very few children outside and Flynn can carry out his careful experimentation . . .

Jenelle (a teacher) asks of 7-month-old Neisha, 'What is she trying to tell me?' as the baby shifts her attention from a shell to the camera when

Jenelle tries to record a 'great first moment'. Jenelle passes the camera to Neisha and later asks 'What am I doing passing a digital camera to a baby to explore?' and 'What can she learn from this experience?' Later, learning stories in Neisha's portfolio document further examples of her exploration of objects as she grows older and more mobile. Jenelle's questions begin to be answered with hindsight.

Mana reo – communication. A key teacher recognises a child's languages

The teachers develop ways to be in tune with the communication of the infants. Writing about Ruby crawling from the outside area up a ramp, Lorraine (one of the teachers) comments:

> She seemed to by-pass our new natural infant garden, of such interest to others, in favour of that long haul directly up the ramp and inside . . . I knew on that first day (as she crawled from the infant house into the toddler space a considerable distance away) that she knew she'd achieved a worthy goal – her whole body language conveyed this without me having to double guess and if I needed any further proof it was the way she explored in that spot for a very long time.

Greerton have a 'key teacher' strategy at both centres, for the infants and toddlers, and the older children too. In this way they recognise a child's main languages (using language in the widest sense to include sounds, gestures, facial expressions and body movement) – and, they add, the 'dialects' too.

Rachel (another teacher) says to pre-speaking Ruby, 'Would you like me to read that story to you Ruby?' And she adds 'Well, there was no maybe about it. It was a straight-up, simple 'No'!' Key teachers' intimate knowledge of a child underpins their ability to interpret children's intentions.

Mana Tangata – contribution. Opportunities and places for collaborative work are deliberately set up

A sense of 'what is fair in this place' is a thread embedded in the culture of learning and teaching at Greerton. Rules are not imposed; rather, there is a teasing out, a negotiation about what feels right. Kindness is a valued action and there are many examples of children thoughtfully supporting each other. The environment is structured to nurture this and there are comfortable places, designed for children, both inside and outside – where, for example, toddler Ruby could 'read' a book to another child –

and a number of places where situations could be deliberately developed (by teachers and by children) so that children needed help from each other, such as negotiating a wheelbarrow across a narrow plank bridge. Collaborative work is documented because teachers understand the power of documentation to support children's identities as strong and capable learners who help each other. This identity is further strengthened as children revisit and share their stories of kindness, thoughtfulness and team work with each other and with their families.

Some illustrative outcomes from Te Whāriki for this curriculum principle

Table 4.1 provides examples taken from Te Whāriki explanations of ngā honongā/relationships and the indicative outcomes from the strands. The curriculum strands are nouns. The learning outcomes include verbs or actions that can be observed: for instance, developing knowledge and understanding, discovering, discussing, negotiating and disagreeing. These actions often fit more than one of the strands, reflecting the connected and woven aspects of teaching and learning.

Table 4.1 Ngā honongā/relationships

Curriculum strands	Learning outcomes. Children develop:
Belonging – Mana whenua	Knowledge about the features of the area of physical and spiritual significance to the local community, such as the local river or mountain;
	An understanding of the links between the early childhood education setting and the known and familiar wider world through people, images, objects, languages, sounds, smells and tastes that are the same as home;
	Interest and pleasure in discovering an unfamiliar wider world where the people, images, objects, languages, sounds, smells and tastes are different from those at home;
	The capacity to discuss and negotiate rules, rights and fairness;
	The ability to disagree and state a conflicting opinion assertively and appropriately.
Well-being – Mana atua	A growing capacity to tolerate and enjoy a moderate degree of change, surprise, uncertainty and puzzling events;

Table 4.1 Continued

Curriculum strands	Learning outcomes. Children develop:
	Confidence and the ability to express emotional needs and trust that their emotional needs will be responded to;
	A sense of responsibility for their own well-being and that of others.
Exploration – Mana aotūroa	Confidence with moving in space, moving to rhythm, and playing near and with others;
	The ability to identify and use information from a range of sources, including using books for reference.
Communication – Mana reo	The confidence and ability to express their ideas and to assist others;
	The ability to disagree and state a conflicting opinion assertively and appropriately;
	Language skills for increasingly complex purposes (these are listed, page 76);
	The inclination to listen attentively and respond appropriately to others.
Contribution – Mana tangata	A sense of 'who they are', their place in the wider world of relationships, and the ways in which these are valued;
	Strategies and skills for initiating, maintaining, and enjoying a relationship with other children (these are listed, page 70) in a variety of contexts;
	An understanding of their own rights and those of others;
	The ability to recognise discriminatory practices and behaviour and to respond appropriately;
	Respect for children who are different from themselves and ease of interaction with them;
	An increasing ability to take another's point of view and to empathise with others;
	A sense of responsibility and respect for the needs and well-being of the group, including taking responsibility for group decisions.

Key points

1. One of the principles in Te Whāriki is that children learn through responsive and reciprocal relationships with people, places, and things.
2. The curriculum document Te Whāriki emphasises belonging, participation, and community.

3. 'Sustained shared thinking' is one aspect of responsive and reciprocal relationships with *people*.
4. Responsive and reciprocal relationships with *places* may refer to an actual place but may also have metaphorical meaning.
5. Responsive and reciprocal relationships with *things* taps into the literature on the role of artefacts in education and in museum collections.
6. In Te Whāriki, the learning outcomes are indicative rather than definitive; they turn the nouns (belonging, well-being, exploration, communication and contribution) into verbs or actions.

Reflective questions

- What reading about relationships has influenced you? And, having read it, what difference did it make to your thinking?
- Read Figure 4.1 (Tangata!) again. What learning do you think was happening here?
- Read Figure 4.2 (Eden the builder) again. What stories about children engaging with things and 'real life' problems come to mind?
- Thinking about the case study. In the early childhood centre you know best:
  - what opportunities are there for children to plan modifications to the programme?
  - what stories of playfulness and joy can you recollect?
  - what routines are in place and does the balance between routine and focused play work well?
  - How are the children's languages recognised and strengthened?
  - What opportunities are there for collaborative work?

References

Carr, M. (2011) Young children reflecting on their learning: teachers' conversations strategies. *Early Years* 31(3), 257–70.

Cowie, B. (2000) Formative assessment in science classrooms. PhD thesis. Hamilton: University of Waikato.

Groundwater-Smith, S., Cusworth, R. and Dobbins, R. (1998) *Behaving Ethically in Teaching: Challenges and Dilemmas.* Marrickville: Harcourt Brace (pp.297–306).

Hargreaves, A. and Moore, S. (2000) Educational outcomes, modern and postmodern interpretations: response to Smyth and Dow. *British Journal of Sociology of Education,* 21(1), 27–42.

Lave, J. (1996) Teaching, as learning, in practice. *Mind, Culture, and Activity,* 3(3), 149–64.

McKergow, F. and Taylor, K. (2011) *Te Hau Nui. The Great Catch: Object Stories from the Manawa.* Auckland: Random House.

Mason, J. (2002) *Researching Your Own Practice: The Discipline of Noticing.* London: RoutledgeFalmer.

Massey, D. (2005) *For Space.* London: Sage.

Melbourne, H. (2009) *Te Wao Nui a Tane.* Wellington: Huia.

Mercer, N. and Littleton, K. (2007) *Dialogue and the Development of Children's Thinking: A Sociocultural Approach.* London: Routledge.

Moss, P. (2007) Meeting across the paradigmatic divide. *Educational Philosophy and Theory,* 39(3), 229–45.

Pahl, K. and Rowsell, J. (2010) *Artifactual Literacies: Every Object Tells a Story.* New York: Teachers College Press.

Peters, S. (2009) Responsive, reciprocal relationships: the heart of the Te Whaariki curriculum. In T. Papatheodorou and J. Moyles (eds), *Learning Together in the Early Years: Exploring Relational Pedagogy* (pp.24–35). London: Routledge.

Robinson, P. and Bartlett, C. (2011) 'Stone crazy': a space where intentional teachers and intentional learners meet. *Early Childhood Folio,* 15(2), 10–14.

Simpson, M. and Williams, T. (2011) Te tuangi (the clam): a metaphor for teaching and learning and the key competencies. *Early Childhood Folio,* 15(2), 4–9.

Siraj-Blatchford, I. (2010) A focus on pedagogy: case studies of effective practice. In K. Sylva, E. Melhuish, P. Sammons, I. Siraj-Blatchford and B. Taggart (eds), *Early Childhood Matters: Evidence from the Effective Pre-school and Primary Education Project.* (pp.149–65). London: Routledge.

Sylva, K., Melhuish, E., Sammons, P., Siraj-Blatchford, I. and Taggart, B. (eds), (2010) *Early Childhood Matters: Evidence from the Effective Pre-school and Primary Education Project.* London: Routledge.

Wattchow, B. and Brown, M. (2011) *A Pedagogy of Place: Outdoor Education for a Changing World.* Clayton, Vic.: Monash University Publishing

Wertsch, J. (1998) *Mind as Action.* New York: Oxford University Press.

Whitty, P. (2009) Towards designing a postfoundational curriculum document. In L. Ianacci and P. Whitty (eds), *Early Childhood Curricula: Reconceptualist Perspectives* (pp.35–62). Calgary: Detselig Enterprises.

5 | Principle two: Kotahitanga/ holistic development

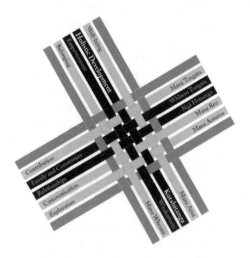

This means, for us, that children are recognised as complex individuals who carry much prior learning and knowledge and skills, different global experiences, languages, cultures and religions. They command respect. All of these, and many more, make up the child's complexity. The only way through this multi-layered complexity is to develop meaningful respectful relationships with the child and family. And to recognise that there is also a wider community involved. This takes time. We will never know all. However, we can be aware and listen for the learning that children and families will whisper and share with us (Teacher reflection, Robyn).

The second of the four foundation principles guiding teaching, learning and purpose in Te Whāriki is kotahitanga/holistic development. The introduction to this principle in the document (p.41) says 'The early childhood curriculum reflects the holistic way children learn and grow'.

It refers back to the weaving metaphor to add that 'cognitive, social, cultural, physical, emotional, and spiritual dimensions of human development are integrally interwoven'. Te Whāriki outlines the ways in which this interconnection and interweaving occur. Learning and development will be integrated through:

- tasks, activities and contexts that have meaning for the child, including practices and activities not always associated with the word 'curriculum', such as care routines, mealtimes, and child management strategies;
- opportunities for open-ended exploration and play;
- consistent, warm relationships that connect everything together;
- recognition of the spiritual dimension of children's lives in culturally, socially and individually appropriate ways;
- recognition of the significance and contribution of previous generations to the child's concept of self.

Here we outline four sites of reflection about curriculum development and implementation with ngā honongā/holistic development in mind: the image of the child, the image of the good society, inclusive practices and valued outcomes.

Image of the child: as dependant, as learner, as citizen

In a paper about the role of the image of the child in policy-making, Linda (Mitchell, 2010) has set out three categories of the image of the child: child as dependant, child as learner and child as citizen. The child as dependant is constructed as the private responsibility of parents, except where parents cannot provide. The child as learner, within a community of learners, emphasises ECE as a learning environment, focused on the child and incorporating family contributions in the interests of children's learning and well-being. The child as citizen positions the child as a member of a social group and wider community, with rights in mind. The purpose of ECE here is to support the society's flourishing. She has linked these to policy directions, and they can also be linked to the curriculum. This is another valuable topic for discussion and debate about the curriculum. It is not merely a technical matter; it is centrally about the image of the child.

In 2009 Angela Anning commented that in spite of the principles underpinning the image of the child in the Early Foundation Stage in the UK – as a unique child with positive relationships, enabling environments and learning and development (Department for Education and Skills, 2007) – 'the 'standards agenda' lobby still has a powerful hold on government policy for early years education' in the UK (p.69). She elaborates on this as follows:

> policy imperatives based on 'universality', 'standardisation' and the measurement of 'quality' using schedules that finally reduce all judgements of both children and workers in pre-school settings to crude numerical outcomes (p.68).

The standards agenda lobby that Anning refers to is lurking at the edges of government policy for early childhood education in a number of countries in the twenty-first century, and Aotearoa New Zealand is no exception.

The Figure 5.1 teaching and learning episode, 'A mermaid costume', illustrates the notion of the child as a learner grappling with the 'risky business' of learning as Julie, the teacher, comments. It describes a task that appears to have great meaning for Samantha: drawing a plan and then sewing a mermaid costume. The teacher describes Samantha as being a learner 'on the edge of mastery' who 'didn't give up', tries new things and persists with difficulty. This image of a learner is clearly described for the child (and for the family who will read this story). The teacher and another child are deliberately supporting the development of these qualities. Could this be reduced to numerical outcomes?

Image of the good society

On the page of Te Whāriki opposite the Bronfenbrenner discussion of the role of several levels of context for the curriculum, there are paragraphs that comment on the changing role of families, increasing cultural diversity and a rapidly changing society. These comments include the following extract:

> The early childhood curriculum supports the cultural identity of all children, affirms and celebrates cultural differences, and aims to help children gain a positive awareness of their own and other cultures . . . New Zealand is part of a world

A mermaid costume

Mermaids have been big at Stanmore Bay Kindergarten for a while now. Lots of wonderful dramatic play has been happening and the transformation of girl into mermaid through some cleverly tied on pieces of fabric! I invited the mermaids to make their own mermaid costumes today, and stage one was to draw a plan. Samantha was keen and I sat and drew alongside her.

She drew the hair first, then the eyes and the mouth. "This mermaid is a little bit grumpy!" she said when looking at her drawing. She started to lose her courage after the face. "I can't draw mermaids – can you draw one for me?" I declined and suggested instead to help her to draw by talking her through the various parts. Samantha managed the neck and shoulders but when it came to the tail she was clearly unimpressed by her own attempt and was on the verge of giving up. "You'll only get better at drawing if you practice." I said and urged her to keep trying. Stephanie was very encouraging and said, "It looks like a good tail to me!"

This cheered Samantha up a bit and soon she made mermaid picture number two. Zaria was drawing a mermaid and I said, "Look, your mermaid tail looks quite like Zaria's one!" This spurred her on, and later we found some fabric and Samantha did a fantastic job of hand sewing. Sewing the material was tough. It's hard pushing the needle through the

Figure 5.1 A mermaid costume

sparkly fabric, but she remained very dedicated to the task. I held the fabric and Samantha sewed. We will continue on with the sewing project when she next comes as we ran out of time today to finish it.

What learning is happening here?

Sometimes learning is a risky business as Guy Claxton, author of many books on teaching and learning, says! As adults we sometimes forget the challenge of learning something new – it's not always easy! Being on the edge of mastery can be a fragile place and challenge our view of ourselves – no matter what age you are! I was really pleased that Samantha didn't give up on her mermaid drawing. I have noticed a greater degree of willingness to try new things and persist with difficulty in Samantha – FANTASTIC!

What's next?

Finish the mermaid costume and see where that leads us!

Figure 5.1 Continued

Written by Julie

revolution in communication, technology, work and leisure. Change in these and other spheres is a feature of everyday life. To cope with such changes, children need both the confidence to develop their own perspectives and the capacity to continue acquiring new knowledge and skills (Te Whāriki, p.18).

Article 29 (Aims of Education) of the UN Convention on the Rights of the Child includes two clauses (c) and (d)) that provide values for this aspect of curriculum. Parties to this convention agree that the education of the child shall be directed to:

(a) The development of the child's personality, talents and mental and physical abilities to their fullest potential;
(b) The development of respect for human rights and fundamental freedoms, and for the principles enshrined in the Charter of the United Nations;
(c) The development of respect for the child's parents, his or her own cultural identity, language and values, for the national values of the country in which the child is living, the country from which he or she may originate, and for civilisations different from his or her own;
(d) The preparation of the child for responsible life in a free society, in the spirit of understanding, peace, tolerance, equality of the sexes, and friendship among all peoples, ethnic, national and religious groups and persons of indigenous origin;
(e) The development of respect for the natural environment.

Writing about the development of the Australian Early Years Learning Framework (EYLF), Jennifer Sumsion *et al.* comment that 'Curriculum is not only a reflection of what a society values, but of what it hopes to become' (p.7). They added:

> The development of a curriculum or learning framework inevitably involves risks. During the development of Te Whāriki, for example, the early childhood sector in New Zealand was acutely aware of the potential risk of the 'schoolification' effect of a national curriculum and worked hard to counter that risk (Carr and May, 2000). The EYLF consultation processes revealed similar concerns (Sumsion et al., 2009, p.7).

The framing of the EYLF document 'Belonging, being and becoming' has some similar features to Te Whāriki, as we saw in Chapter 2. It also keeps the notion of a permeable and open-ended curriculum, enabling but not prescribing particular knowledge and skills.

Inclusive practices: weaving holistic development

In an account of one context in which early childhood teachers and early intervention professionals were attempting to co-construct professional knowledge in order to implement an inclusive special education policy, Joy Cullen writes about the debate on 'the place of subject knowledge and skills learning in a holistic curriculum' (Cullen, 2009 p.81). She writes that these professionals were engaged in a complex journey towards inclusion and argues that a critical component of the journey is the shared construction of professional knowledge. She argues that co-construction (the relationship principle, discussed in Chapter 4) should also apply to the shared meaning-making of educators, early intervention professionals and other stakeholders involved in provision for young children with special needs. Research data had continued to reveal concerns from educators about an excessive focus on the isolated teaching of skills in individual education plans. She suggests (p.83) that a way forward, consistent with sociocultural theory and integrating skills and interests, is the narrative assessment (learning stories) that has been developed alongside Te Whāriki. Chapter 8 will say more about this assessment practice. In the context of inclusion, Joy Cullen summarises the view of Lesley Dunn (2002), a psychologist working in early intervention, who has described the application of learning stories in early intervention as a way to promote inclusion. She outlines many of its advantages, including:

- data are collected in natural contexts;
- the environment in which learning takes place is described, including the roles of peers and caregivers;
- programmes derived from learning story assessment can work with the child's strengths and pinpoint where the child begins to have difficulty (Cullen, 2009, p.84).

Cullen concludes that 'the sociocultural lens is a powerful means of viewing the journey towards inclusion' (p.90). In an earlier paper she set out three sets of rights for inclusion in a programme that reflects sociocultural principles: the child's right to belong, the child's right to share interests, and the child's right for differences to be acknowledged and respected. Lesley Dunn had added a fourth: the right to be seen in the same way as everyone else. In Te Whāriki, the right to belong is both a strand of outcome and, in effect, a fourth principle: family and community, the topic of Chapter 6.

Valued outcomes: working theories and learning dispositions

Chapter 4 introduced some of the characteristics of outcomes in Te Whāriki. The curriculum names three features of these outcomes: they are indicative rather than prescriptive; each setting will develop their own emphases and priorities for the teaching of these outcomes, and the outcomes integrate 'working theories' and learning dispositions:

> The outcomes of a curriculum are knowledge, skills and attitudes. The list of outcomes in this document is indicative rather than definitive. Each early childhood education setting will develop its own emphases and priorities. In early childhood, holistic, active learning and the total process of learning are emphasised. Knowledge, skills, and attitudes are closely linked. These three aspects combine to form a child's 'working theory' and help the child develop dispositions that encourage learning (p.44).

The curriculum explains:

> In early childhood, children are developing more elaborate and useful working theories about themselves and about the people, places and things in their lives. These working theories contain a combination of knowledge about the world, skills and strategies, attitudes and expectations . . . The second way in which knowledge, skills and attitudes combine is as dispositions – 'habits of mind' or 'patterns of learning'.

These habits of mind or dispositions are characterised as having three parts: inclination, skills and a sensitivity to occasion or an attunement to opportunity, or being able to read an environment for opportunities in it (see David Perkins *et al.*'s (1993) three-part analysis of 'thinking dispositions'). The book *Making Learning Whole* (Perkins, 2009) is relevant to this chapter. The curriculum (p.44) provides as an example the disposition to be curious and the three parts are:

- an inclination to enjoy puzzling over events;
- the skills to ask questions about them in different ways;

■ an understanding of when is the most appropriate time to ask these questions

Since this document was published there has been considerable interest in working theories and dispositions that encourage learning, and the relationship between them. Sally Peters and Keryn Davis (2012) and Helen Hedges (2011) have researched this topic, and two of the authors of this book (Carr and Lee, 2012) have described learning in early childhood education as appropriating interconnected stores of disposition and stores of knowledge. Figure 5.2 includes two conversations and a sketch from a group of kindergarten children who are visiting the exhibition 'Unveiled: 200 years of wedding fashion' at Te Papa Tongawera, the National Museum of Aotearoa New Zealand. This exhibition was on loan from the Victoria and Albert Museum in London. The children are sharing their working theories and ideas about the size of a wedding dress, a prince and the dangerous nature of weddings. They are also making connections between what they sketch at the museum and how this might be reified[1] in a book back at the centre.

Another term for what is being learned, in a holistic sense, is 'repertoires of practice'. Kris Gutiérrez and Barbara Rogoff, writing about a project that brought high school students from migrant farmworker backgrounds to the University of California, describe a 4-week summer residential programme with a 'rich curriculum, dense with learning activity organised around sociocultural views of learning and development' (2008, p.148):

> Briefly, traditional notions of development generally define change along a vertical dimension, moving, for example, from immaturity and incompetence to maturity and competence . . . A more expansive view of development also is concerned with the horizontal forms of expertise that develop within and across an individual's practices . . . I believe the notion of repertoires of practice captures both vertical and horizontal forms of expertise (Gutiérrez and Rogoff, 2003); this includes not only what students learn in formal learning environments such as schools, but also what they learn by participating in a range of practices outside of school (Gutiérrez and Rogoff, 2008, p.149).

A repertoire of practice that combines stores of knowledge and dispositions, and links to practices outside the early childhood setting, is illustrated by a comment by Fran, a teacher who introduces the next chapter:

Sharing ideas and working theories at a museum

Dylan, Madiba and Y were looking carefully at an embroidered black silk wedding dress (Qui a droit? Christian Lacroix Haute Couture 1993–4).

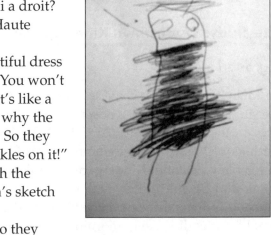

Y: "That's a beautiful dress with sparkles on it. You won't believe your eyes, it's like a treasure. You know why the black one is so big? So they can put lots of sparkles on it!" (The children sketch the exhibit: see Madiba's sketch here).

Madiba: "Why do they wear a veil? To make them beautiful for a prince."

Dylan: "I've been a ring bearer. I wore a suit like that one (pointing). But it was black not sparkly."

Madiba: "That suit is called a tuxedo."

Dylan: "We can take our drawings and laminate them to make a book at kindy!"

Maiangi (teacher), Ben, Dylan and Madiba are watching a film of Prince Charles' and Lady Di's wedding. Prince Charles wears a wide blue sash and a sword.

Madiba: "Who's the guy in blue?"

Dylan: "The Principal."

Maiangi: "The prince? Prince Charles?"

Someone nearby points out Prince Charles' sword.

Ben explains, "There are baddies at weddings sometimes."

Figure 5.2 Sharing ideas and working theories at a museum

Written by Maiangi and Becs

One particular way in which I think holistic development is supported at our centre is the way in which ideas around recycling and sustainability are interwoven into the programme. Children and their families contribute materials that are used at our recycling station. The exploration of these materials and the way in which they support children's learning quests reflects an environment that values learning that is not only about acquiring skills but one that is connected to developing understandings and an awareness of the surrounding world (Fran).

A case study: Wadestown Kindergarten

Background

Wadestown Kindergarten is the second of five Centres of Innovation case studies in Chapters 4 to 7. Wadestown Kindergarten was a designated Centre of Innovation from 2006 to 2009. The kindergarten nestles in the hills of Wadestown, a suburb of Wellington, the capital city of Aotearoa New Zealand. Kindergarten families are mainly of high socio-economic and Pākehā background, with some children of British, Māori, Niuean and Indian ethnicities. The kindergarten is sessional, with thirty 4-year-olds attending five mornings a week and thirty 3-year-olds attending in the afternoon, three sessions a week. When it became a Centre of Innovation the staff team included two qualified and registered teachers and a teacher aide employed in the afternoons. A little over a year later a third qualified and registered teacher joined the team.

The research focus of Wadestown Kindergarten was on investigating multimodal literacies and their roles in communicative competence and meaning-making. The teachers came to define literacies broadly within their study as modes of communication, conceptualisation and meaning-making. The following examples of opportunities for a holistic approach to curriculum come from a publication describing some of the practices at the kindergarten (Mitchell *et al.*, 2009) and from the final report.

Mana Atua – well-being. Making a grandmother welcome

One of the teachers, Yvette, reflects as follows:

Jacqui had just started kindergarten and her grandmother came with her every day to help her settle into this new space. Grandma Betty had a keen interest in crafts and helped out at the children's programme at the local church. She suggested that she could bring crafts in to do with the children, as a way to be present for Jacqui and also to help out throughout the sessions . . . Over the following weeks and months we began to notice the way that not only Jacqui responded to Grandma Betty's presence (in terms of her feeling safe at kindergarten) but also how other children began to value her presence . . . She would often tailor her craft-making activities to fit in with the children's interests, e.g. during a project on the 'jungle', she made animal masks with the group.

Mana aotūroa – exploration. Meaning-making in multiple modes

Multiple literacies, in this case drawing, writing and graphic conventions, interrelate with and support each other. Having a broad conception of literacies allows for a greater range of possibilities for children and does not marginalise children whose literacy strengths may be different from those of many other children. Miro's use of the graphic convention of the thought bubble, taught to her by her mum, enables her to bring additional dimensions of action and reflection into her drawing. In this way the drawing features a combining of modes; Susan Wright (2007) refers to this as children's proclivity to cross channels of communication. Further crossover occurs as Miro combines drawing with writing. The combination of drawing and writing is one that Wright notes is very common in many young children's drawings. In Miro's pictures she identifies herself by positioning her name above the figure.

Mana whenua – belonging. Pedagogy around projects

Wadestown Kindergarten encourages projects emerging from children's interests that extend over time and allow a purposeful focus that connects curriculum strands. The willingness of adults to offer opportunities for children to follow their interests in a single-minded and impassioned way *across different contexts* also connects principles and strands and enriches the definition of literacy. They thus support children to develop competency in a literacy mode.

Mana tangata – contribution. The contributions of children, teachers and families are woven together

The Wadestown research team explained their use of a woven wall hanging as a metaphor for:

the way we envisage multiple literacies helping facilitate the contributions of our learning community to the curriculum whāriki. The vertical strands of the weaving . . . represent multiple literacies. Through these strands the contributions of children, teachers and families are woven. The more literacies (vertical strands) used, the more extended this enables contributions to be with each strand serving to support others (Simonsen *et al.*, 2010, p.2).

One of the transformations at the kindergarten was to make it possible for parents to contribute more to interpreting children's learning and development, where the traditional role of the teacher as the expert in this field was replaced by a teacher who was open to learning from the insights and experiences of parents and whānau.

Mana reo – communication. A popular practice of list-making

Writing's permanency and usefulness as a memory aid is capitalised on at Wadestown Kindergarten in the popular practice of list-making. Lists are often used to establish the sequence of turns. In one instance the list is drawn up for taking turns on the red and blue bikes and one of the children, Hugo, came up with the idea of writing the words 'red' and 'blue' in colour, a useful strategy for helping children work out which list to put themselves on. Hugo's idea to combine colour coding and alphabetic writing provides a simple example of the way different codes can be brought together to complement and support each other. Another child, Elizabeth, suggests crossing people's names out once they had finished their turn. This diagram-like strategy involves a further departure from purely alphabetic writing. The list is a collaborative interweaving of visual and spatial as well as written elements, an illustration of Carey Jewitt and Gunther Kress's (2002) point that communication is more than words.

Figure 5.3, not from this case study, illustrates a baby's holistic 'lantern consciousness', a 'vivid panoramic illumination of the everyday' (Gopnik, 2009, p.129).

Learning to move

Today I spent some time in the infant whare on the floor with my new friend Harrison. I have greeted him and watched his face slowly light up in a smile in past weeks, but often he has been in Lynnette's arms or in his capsule ready to go home. However, today I sat down with him on the carpet to keep him company while Rachel prepared his milk. And what a joy it was! Harrison you looked at me with such trust and a calm interest, not batting an eyelid when I brought over the camera and began recording these moments for you. I was fascinated to watch you repeat patterns of movement, over and over again you flexed and extended your arms and legs as if that, in itself, was a way to communicate curiosity and contentment.

What learning was happening?

By lying on the firm surface of the floor you are exploring some of the ways that your body is able to move. Not only that, at the same time you are taking in all the happenings around you through your senses – you see a new face appearing above you, you hear a familiar voice

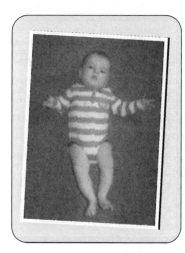

Figure 5.3 Learning to move

speaking somewhere across the room. So many aspects of being alive and awake! Alison Gopnik speaks of the "lantern consciousness" of infants (she defines infants as children under the age of 5 yrs), who have not yet developed the capacity of filtering out aspects of their environment to focus on one chosen area. So while you are moving and experiencing your body, how it fills the space around you, you are also processing information on the sights, sounds, temperature, tactile aspects of your clothes, the carpet etc, smells in the air, what it is like to meet and greet a less familiar person. No wonder you need to sleep after a while!

Harrison, I so enjoyed these moments I had with you. You happily let me into your world of new discoveries and I look forward to watching your journey unfold.

Figure 5.3 Continued

Written by Kate

Some illustrative outcomes from Te Whāriki for this curriculum principle

Table 5.1 provides examples taken from Te Whāriki explanations of kotahitanga/holistic development and the indicative outcomes from the strands. The interconnection of the strands can be illustrated here. Readers may want to place the outcomes in more than one category of the strand and add their own. This is another opportunity for reflection, ensuring that the meanings of learning and the purposes of teaching in early childhood continue to be a subject of recontextualising discussion and debate.

Table 5.1 Kotahitanga/holistic development

Curriculum strands	Learning outcomes. Children develop:
Belonging – Mana whenua	An awareness of connections between events and experiences within and beyond the early childhood education setting;
	A feeling of belonging, and having a right to belong, in the early childhood setting;
	An ability to take on different roles in different contexts;
	An understanding of the rules of the early childhood education setting, of the reasons for them, and of which rules will be different in other settings.
Well-being – Mana atua	A sense of personal worth, and knowledge that personal worth does not depend on today's behaviour or ability;
	An ability to identify their own emotional responses and those of others.
Exploration – Mana aotūroa	Confidence in using a variety of strategies for exploring and making sense of the world; A perception of themselves as 'explorers' – competent, confident learners who ask questions and make discoveries;
	The ability to enquire, research, explore, generate, and modify their own working theories about the natural, social, physical, and material worlds.
Communication – Mana reo	Familiarity with an appropriate selection of the stories and literature valued by the cultures in their community.
	Experience with creating stories and symbols;
	Familiarity with print and its uses by exploring and observing the use of print in activities that have meaning and purpose for children;
	An ability to be creative and expressive through a variety of activities, such as pretend play, carpentry, storytelling, drama, and making music.
Contribution – Mana tangata	Some early concepts of the value of appreciating diversity and fairness;
	Abilities and interests in a range of domains – spatial, visual, linguistic, physical, logical or mathematical, personal and social – which build on children's strengths;
	An appreciation of the ways in which they can make contributions to groups and to group well-being.

Key points

1. The principle of holistic development in Te Whāriki is 'The early childhood curriculum reflects the holistic way children learn and grow'. Learning and development can be integrated through
   - tasks, activities and contexts that have meaning for the child;
   - opportunities for open-ended exploration and play;
   - consistent, warm relationships that connect everything together;
   - recognition of the spiritual dimension of children's lives in culturally, socially, and individually appropriate ways;
   - recognition of the significance and contribution of previous generations to the child's concept of self.
2. The image of the child in an early childhood setting is influential: children can be seen as dependants, learners and citizens. These can be linked to policy decisions and they are also relevant to the way we teach.
3. The image of the good society also influences the curriculum in a setting.
4. Inclusive practices provide holistic environments for children.
5. Working theories and learning dispositions summarise the valued outcomes in Te Whāriki.

Reflective questions

- When you think of a child as a learner, what comes to mind? How does that image influence teaching?
- When you think of a child as a citizen, what comes to mind? How does that image influence teaching?
- Read Figure 5.3 (Learning to move) again. Think about the image of the child represented here. How did this image influence Kate's response?
- Think about the case study. In the early childhood centre you know best:
  - What opportunities are there for meaning-making by the children in different modes on the same topic or interest?
  - Share projects by groups of children that seem to have been successful.
  - Are families able to make a contribution to the early childhood programme?

- What literacies are available?
- What opportunities are there for collaborative work?
- What reading about children's projects or working theories or learning dispositions has influenced you? And, having read it, what difference did it make to your thinking?
- Read Figure 5.1 (The mermaid costume) again. Did something capture your interest in this?
- Read the conversations in Figure 5.2 (Sharing ideas and working theories and connections at a museum) again. What working theories and learning dispositions are exemplified here? Share any early years sustained conversations that you remember. What sustained them?

Note

1   Reification is the process that Wenger (1998, p. 57) says captures the transformation of a process into an object that can establish it as an enduring commitment and enables it to be revisited and discussed by the community. He argues that a curriculum document is a very good example of this.

References

Anning, A. (2009) The co-construction of an early childhood curriculum. In A. Anning, J. Cullen and M. Fleer (eds), *Early Childhood Education. Society and Culture* (pp.67–79). London: Sage.

Cullen, J. (2009) Adults co-constructing professional knowledge. In A. Anning, J. Cullen and M. Fleer (eds), *Early Childhood Education: Society and Culture* (pp.80–90). London: Sage.

Department for Education and Skills (2007) *The Early Years Foundation Stage: Setting the Standards for Learning, Development and Care for Children from Birth to Five*. Nottingham: DfES.

Dunn, L. (2002) Children with special rights. *Early Education, 30* (spring/summer), 17–22.

Gopnik, A. (2009) *The Philosophical Baby: What Children's Minds Tell Us about Truth, Love and the Meaning of Life*. New York: Farrar, Straus and Giroux.

Gutiérrez, K. D. and Rogoff, B. (2008) Developing a sociocritical literacy in the third space. *Reading Research Quarterly, 43*(2), 148–64.

Hedges, H. (2011) Connecting 'snippets of knowledge': teachers' understandings of the concept of working theories. *Early Years, 31*(3), 271–84.

Jewitt, C. and Kress, G. (2002) More than words: the construction of scientific entities though image, gesture and movement in the science classroom. In J. Koppen, I. Lunt and C. Wulf (eds), *Education in Europe, Cultures, Values, Institutions in Transition* (pp. 225–45). Berlin: Waxmann.

Mitchell, L. (2010) Constructions of childhood in early childhood education policy in New Zealand. *Contemporary Issues in Early Childhood Education*, 11(4), 328–41.

Mitchell, L., Simonsen, Y. and Haggerty, M. (2009) Finding out about children's literacies in family contexts: vignettes from Wadestown Kindergarten. *Early Childhood Folio*, 13, 16–21.

Perkins, D. (2009) *Making Learning Whole: How Seven Principles of Teaching can Transform Education*. San Francisco, CA: Jossey-Bass.

Perkins, D., Tishman, S., Richhart, R., Donis, K. and Andrade, A. (1993) Beyond abilities: a dispositional theory of thinking. *Merrill-Palmer Quarterly*, 39(1), 1–21.

Peters, S. and Davis, K. (2012) Working theories and learning dispositions in early childhood education: perspectives from New Zealand. In T. Papatheodorou (ed.) *International Debates on Early Childhood Practices and Policies* (pp.148–58). London: Routledge.

Simonsen, Y., Blake, M., LaHood, A., Haggerty, M., Mitchell, L. and Wray, L. (2010) A curriculum whāriki of multimodal literacies. Retrieved from http://www.education counts.govt.nz/publications/ece/22551/70769/71393.

Sumison, J., Cheeseman, S., Kennedy, A., Barnes, S., Harrison, L. and Stonehouse, A. (2009) Insider perspectives on developing belonging, being and becoming: the early years learning framework for Australia. *Australasian Journal of Early Childhood*, 34(4), 4–13.

Wright, S. (2007) Young children's meaning making through drawing and 'telling'. Analogies to filmic textual features. *Australian Journal of Early Childhood*, 32(4), 37–48.

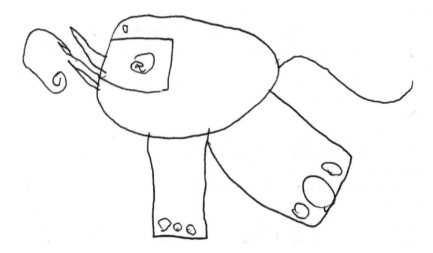

<table>
<tr><td>

6

</td><td>

Principle three: Whakamana/ empowerment

</td></tr>
</table>

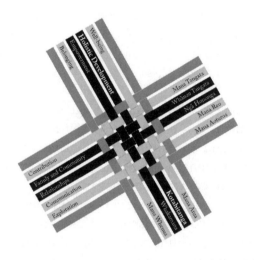

I believe that we trust children to be not only active participants in decision-making but also to really encourage a sense of shared leadership to evolve. Leadership skills are central to the programme and as a result children are encouraged to source others' expertise in a particular area. This offers children a sense of empowerment and places value on this particular way of thinking and learning (Teacher reflection, Fran).

Whakamana is, for the purposes of Te Whāriki, about being empowered, strengthened. All the curriculum strands begin with the stem, *mana*. The strands: mana atua – well-being, mana whenua – belonging, mana aotūroa – exploration, mana reo – communication and mana tangata – contribution have all been expressed as realms of *mana* or sources of strength for sustaining children's lifelong learning journeys: the domains of the spiritual, of land or place, of language, and the world of light, nature and people. The English parallel of mana atua is 'well-being', which does not necessarily encompass the spiritual dimension, so significant in *mana atua* which refers to the gods (atua), godliness, or the spiritual world.

'Whakamana/empowerment' has been elaborated as 'the early childhood curriculum empowers the child to learn and grow'. The emphasis here is on early childhood services assisting children and their families to 'access the resources necessary to enable them to direct their own lives' (Te Whāriki p.40), and, echoing in some measure the United Nations Convention of the Rights of the Child, introduced in Chapter 5, is the following comment (p.40):

> To learn and develop to their potential, children must be respected and valued as individuals. Their rights to personal dignity, to equitable opportunities for participation, to protection from physical, mental, or emotional abuse and injury, and to opportunities for rest and leisure must be safeguarded.

This principle connects with notions of agency and identity. In some curriculum documents it is referred to as 'self-regulation', a label that is more psychological and individual than whakamana/empowerment, in which the concept of agency is more likely to refer to a context. Children are positioned with, or construct, agency in particular contexts, and may begin to recognise or construct these opportunities in other places: to assume the lead or to take responsibility. This is especially true in a classroom or early childhood setting, where sometimes learners can develop their own projects and choose their own activities, and frequently they work, play or talk together within a collective. Different settings will strike different balances with this. The collective and reciprocal vision of Te Whāriki implies that even when children are in charge of their own agenda, they will be expected to watch out for the agency of others as well, as Fran comments in the quote that opens this chapter.

Designing an empowering educational environment

Empowering or powerful educational environments are described in Guy Claxton's (2002) book *Building Learning Power: Helping Young People Become Better Learners*. This work includes many strategies that are helpful to teachers to strengthen children's 'learning muscles' (see also

Claxton *et al.* (2011). During the 1990s Mihaly Csikszentmihalyi and his students at the University of Chicago videotaped interviews with a group of 91 'exceptional' individuals, including 14 Nobel prize winners. They were especially interested in creativity. Csikszentmihalyi (1996) comments: 'while these people may not have been precocious in their achievements in their early years, they seem to have become committed early to the exploration and discovery of some part of their world' (p.158). He has this to say about what features of their early years shaped their creative lives:

> According to this view, a creative life is still determined, but what determines it is a will moving across time – the fierce determination to succeed, to make sense of the world, to use whatever means to unravel some of the mysteries of the universe . . . So where does this fierce determination, this unquenchable curiosity come from? Perhaps that question is too reductionistic to be useful . . . It may not be so important to know precisely where the seeds come from. What *is* important is to recognize the interest when it shows itself, nurture it, and provide the opportunities for it to grow into a creative life (p.182).[1]

School often leaves children to face alone the task of reconciling the 'basic dilemma of educational systems, which must both socialize learners into the social order and give them the means to change that social order' (Kramsch, 1993, p.236). In Chapter 4 we saw that at Greerton Early Childhood Centre children are included in the planning of the outdoor area. In *Listening to Young Children*, Alison Clark and Peter Moss (2011) have provided a number of examples of consultation with children on topics that matter; so has the edited book *Children's Voices: Research, Policy and Practice* by Anne Smith *et al.* (2000).

Included here is an example of listening to children's viewpoints from a kōhanga reo (see Soutar and Te Whānau o Mana Tamariki, 2010). It is a paki ako, the adaptation of a learning story in this kōhanga context. It was written in Māori, and has been translated into English for this book. In Figure 6.1 Rea is in conversation with the children after the kōhanga was vandalised. In documenting the story she recognises that although they are all angry, the children were 'guided by their cultural practices and values'. The children talk about the atua and the ancestors, represented on panels in the entrance, rather than focusing on the vandal. They see the vandalism as disrespect to the community and the building.

The act of a rascal!

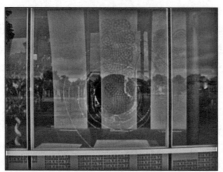

When we came back to kōhanga reo on Monday, we saw that our home had been vandalised by some rascal, by some people up to mischief over the weekend! The cheek, it was a shameless act!

I showed you all the window and the rock that had been thrown to break the window. It really was quite a big rock wasn't it?

"Uuuuuuuu!" some of you sighed. You were cross and I heard the anger in your voices! "By gollly, those rascals!" you said, Te Atahaia. I was in full agreement with you. It's natural we want to punish those responsible! I thought how ignorant

they were. But you lot, you are guided by your cultural practices and values.

"We look after our building because our building always looks after us when our parents bring us here, isn't that right?" you asked me, Te Atahaia.

"Yes, we always love and care for the building, don't we?" you said, Raukura in full support of your friend

I said to you both, "Why should we look after this building?"

Ohomairangi, you said, "Because our building is Tānemāhuta (personified). He'd be sad if we hurt him."

"We'd be sad too," said Matauri.

"Where is Tānemāhuta? Who is he?" I asked you all.

"At the walls. He's my ancestor," replied Ohomairangi.

How grateful I am for your reflections. They showed such leadership. I sat there carefully listening and thought how deeply knowing you are and how much you care about our beautiful home.

You talked about caring for property, about love and about how one can be hurt by the abusive actions of another. I acknowledge too all of your thoughts about our ancestors and Tānemāhuta.

We owe a lot to the trades people who fixed the damage that day also!

Nō te hokinga ki te kōhanga reo i te Mane, ka kitea i tūkinotia tō tātou kainga e ētahi nanakia, e ētahi haututu i te mutunga wiki! Eī, tō rātou hia kore i whakamā, nē e hoa mā, auare ake!

Nāku te matapihi i whakaatu ki a koutou, me te toka i whiua nā reira i pakaru ai te matapihi. He toka rahi tonu, nē hā?

"Uuuuuuuu!" te auē mai a ētahi. Ko te puku o ngā rae me te haruru o ngā reo whakatakariri! "Pai kare nanakia mā!" tāu Te Atahaia. Kei konā katoa au, e hine. Me whiu te hunga nānā tō tātou kāinga i tūkino ka tika! I mahara au, eī, kātahi te hunga kuare ko rātou! Engari anō koutou, he tamariki whai tikanga.

"Me manaaki tātou i te whare nā te mea ko ia ka tiaki i a tātou i ngā wā katoa. I te wā ka kawe mai ngā mātua i a mātou i ngā ata, nē whāea?" tāu i mea mai ki a au, Te Atahaia.

"Ae, me aroha tātou ki a ia i ngā wā katoa, nē?" tāu Raukura me te tino tautoko i tō hoa.

Ko tāku ki a kōrua, "He aha hoki te take me manaaki e tātou te whare nei?"

Ka mea koe Ohomairangi, "Nā te mea ko Tānemāhuta teˉnei whare. Ka pouri a ia mehemea ka mamae ia."

Figure 6.1 The act of a rascal

"Ka pouri hoki tātou,", tā Matauri.

"Kei whea a Tānemāhuta? Ko wai hoki a ia?" tāku ki a koutou.

"Kei ngā pakitara. Ko ia tōku tipuna," te whakahoki a Ohomairangi.

Mā te aha rā i ngā whakaaro i puta. He whakaaro rangatira! I reira au e āta whakarongo ana. I mahara anō au kātahi te hunga mōhio ko koutou! He hunga whai whakaaro ki tō tātou whare ātaahua.

I puta i a koutou ngā kōrero mō te manaaki i ngā hanga, mō te aroha, mō te pāmamae hoki o tētahi i ngā mahi tōkino a ētahi atu. Ka mihi hoki i ngā whakaaro ki tō tātou tupuna, ki a Tānemāhuta, ki a Tane-whakapiripiri.

Maringanui tātou i te hunga nā rātou ngā mahi a te mórere i whakatikatika!

Figure 6.1 Continued

Written by Rea

In a study of early years education that included Margaret and Wendy as authors (Carr *et al.*, 2010), we researched the way in which, for some children, being positioned as authors of their own learning in their Te Whāriki-based early childhood centre encouraged them to seek out opportunities to have their say about the programme at school. We commented from our observations that

> [w]hen children were deemed to be authoring, we noted in the case study chapters that they were: initiating; enjoying; taking on identities as 'grown-ups', expert readers, writers, soccer players, drivers and artists; deeply engaged in activities often with a high level of affect (excitement, emotion); inclined to communicate their opinions; focused and persevering, 'locking on' to learning; interested and enthusiastic; balancing desires and goals; taking responsibility and taking on the role of a teacher (pp. 202–3).

In a chapter on children initiating and orchestrating projects we highlighted four aspects of educational design that enabled children to initiate learning projects:

- The early childhood centre context provided opportunities for children to learn ways to develop relationships with others in order to orchestrate the smooth running of projects that needed partners.
- Space, time and material props were available for children to develop complex pretend play scripts and other personal or shared projects.
- The children built up a relationship with teachers who made the effort to get to know the children and their families in order to invite their interest and engagement.
- Teachers viewed the children as competent learners who could take responsibility (pp.116–18).

In practice, and in our experience, agency and empowerment is about a *balance*: sharing leadership, balancing power with responsibility, balancing authoring with co-authoring.

A case study: Te Kōhanga Reo o Mana Tamariki

Background

In late 1989 the growing number of Kōhanga Reo (Māori language educational settings for children aged 0–5 years) was enlarged with the establishment by Mana Tamariki Inc of Te Kōhanga Reo o Mana Tamariki under the umbrella of the National Kōhanga Reo Trust. By 1995 we opened a new school – a total immersion Māori language school – Te Kura Kaupapa Māori o Mana Tamariki – for children aged 5 to 17 or 18 years. Relationships developed in Mana Tamariki span more than 16 years, cementing lifelong links between Mana Tamariki children, parents and staff. Our kōhanga reo and our school work collaboratively and exist together in a seamless educational setting. Our main objective is the regeneration of the Māori language and customs in our community.

Mana tangata – contribution. The expression of generosity through customary practices involving welcoming, hosting and reciprocity

For Māori, this strand concerns the way in which we carry out meaningful relationships. It is about responsibility, reciprocity, respect and hospitality. Concepts of manaaki (hosting and caring for others) and whakawhanaungatanga (strengthening familial relationships) are key to this strand. An example of this at Mana Tamariki developed around our response to the Christchurch earthquake in February 2011. The earthquake was the second-deadliest natural disaster recorded in New Zealand. At a magnitude 6.3 on the Richter scale it was extremely powerful, causing widespread damage, killing 185 people and wounding many others. The next day at Mana Tamariki we began with an assembly where we explained the tragedy to the children from both a traditional Māori perspective and a scientific western approach. Later that month, after researching ideas with the children as to how we might support the victims of the earthquake, we took them into the city centre where they sang and performed to the public for donations. The funds collected were counted by the children and then taken to a local bank that was collecting on behalf of Christchurch.

Mana atua – well-being. Ancestral and spiritual connections, acknowledgement of tribal identity

From a Māori perspective, our children, through their ancestral links, are connected through aeons of time to the original source of the Māori world. Some Māori, expert in genealogy, are able to recite their history from the beginning of the Māori world, the primeval parents, the gods and so forth, directly to their own tribal ancestor and from there to their own family. Māori believe all children are born of the gods. It is vital that the child's spiritual connection to all that has gone before is nurtured. At Mana Tamariki we promote a spiritual dimension that is indigenously Māori. We take positive aspects from the spirituality our ancestors practised and impart these teachings to the children so they may remain connected to their ancestors' world-view. Some of these teachings take place when children are taught to recite ruruku kai (acknowledgements made before partaking food) that speak directly to the food, welcoming it and acknowledging the gods from whose domains the food originated. Another is mihimihi (greetings) at the beginning and end of the day. During this time everyone comes together and a child recites their pepehā, a statement of their tribal identity. There is singing and a spiritual acknowledgement said to formally open or close the day.

Mana reo – communication. Protecting and enhancing Māori language

No matter how many activities Māori children participate in and no matter how active they are in their own familial and tribal affairs, without knowing the Māori language they are incomplete and therefore cannot fully express their Māori culture. The language is the key to fully understanding the cultural practices and the unique world-view of Māori. Beyond this, of course, is a desire for each individual child to consolidate their knowledge of their own tribal dialect. Mana Tamariki is a strict total immersion Māori language environment where every child enrolled has at least one adult in the home who has committed to speak Māori only to the child and all others enrolled at Mana Tamariki. This has allowed us to build a Māori-speaking community beyond the physical setting of Mana Tamariki. Because of the demise of the Māori language over decades Mana Tamariki, like most Māori educational settings, has no native speaking Māori staff members and most of the Māori-speaking parents did not grow up with Māori as their first language either. This often results in the children growing past the Māori-speaking adults who care for them. In this context both the child and the adult are learners. It is not unusual at Mana Tamariki for the teacher to document a learning moment where the language structure used by the child is more advanced and complex than that of the teachers. These moments are celebrated and optimised by the adults, who, in the process, acquire a higher level of understanding the language.

Mana aotūroa – exploration. Relationship to place

This strand is about the child's place in the world. For Māori, relationship to place is as important as relationship to people. This strand encourages an environment where children are able to explore their relationship with the places surrounding them, the things they have in common with their environment and things that are different. It requires children to be active members of their community and it requires adults to make time and space for children to carry out meaningful investigation and research. As children build their relationships with place, their knowledge of who they are, and of their own identity in relation to those places, grows. At Mana Tamariki our vegetable garden has become one place where children can carry out research. Their work in the garden and their observations of the plants also allow them to find out about how their own bodies function. Because we have followed the teachings of our ancestors in regard to the way in which we garden, the children's relationship with the garden is underpinned by Māori values and practices that have been adapted for this technical, modern age.

Mana Whenua – belonging. Positioning the child within family, sub-tribe and tribe; a welcome ceremony with the whānau

This strand of Te Whāriki is essentially about the child's relationship with people, places, events and things around them. From a Māori perspective those relationships can span decades, centuries and longer, especially relationships with people and places. This is because the children are positioned within their own whānau (extended family), hapū (sub-tribe) and iwi and with their ancestors. All interactions take place with this in mind and the child cannot be isolated from those connections. The aspirations a family has for their children have been arranged long before the child was conceived. Families maintain active participation in tribal affairs and endeavour to stay connected to their relatives and tribal lands, even when they are living some distance away from them. This active participation ensures the individual remains connected tribally. This is the source of an individual's identity. At Mana Tamariki the welcoming ceremony for all new children is one of the ways in which we assist children and their families to establish a relationship with us. Through this process their sense of belonging develops. When a child starts at Mana Tamariki they are welcomed through the process of pōnhiri (traditional welcoming ceremony). They come with their extended family. The welcoming ceremony is documented as a paki ako (the Mana Tamariki adaptation of a learning story).

Te Kōhanga Reo o Mana Tamariki was selected as a Centre of Innovation in 2008 (Soutar *et al.* 2010).

Some illustrative outcomes from Te Whāriki for this curriculum principle

Table 6.1 provides examples taken from Te Whāriki explanations of whakamana/empowerment and the indicative outcomes from the strands. In this table outcomes from a Māori perspective are added to make connections with the case study (see also Chapter 3 and New Zealand Ministry of Education, 2009).

Table 6.1 Whakamana/empowerment

Curriculum strands	Learning outcomes. Children will:	Outcomes from a Māori perspective
Belonging – Mana whenua	create and act on their own ideas, develop knowledge and skills in areas that interest them, make an increasing number of their own decisions and judgments, display an increasing ability to play an active part in the running of the programme	Māori aspirations here include strengthening in children a deep and meaningful knowledge of who they are from a Māori perspective. This may include assisting them to connect with their tribal identity, their tribal lands and their pepehā (identity statement). When a child is born the umbilical cord and afterbirth are usually buried in a special place at the child's tribal home. Māori believe this secures the bond between children and their origins.
Well-being – Mana atua	develop an enhanced sense of self-worth, identity, confidence and enjoyment, understand their own individual ways of learning and being creative, display an increasing ability to determine their own actions and make their own choices	In this strand children should experience rangimārie (peace/calm), aroha (love/empathy/sorrow) and harikoa (joy) from a Māori perspective. It is also important that they know manaaki (hospitality/hosting of others/looking after others) and atawhai (caring for others). Through these concepts the children's belief in themself is reinforced.
Exploration – Mana aotūroa	learn useful and appropriate ways to find out what they want to know, develop the ability to make decisions, choose their own materials, and set their own problems, take responsibility for their own learning, attain a perception of themselves as 'explorers' – competent, confident learners who ask questions and make discoveries	Children will deepen their understanding that everything has a spiritual connection to all other things and to the origins of the Māori world. It is from this basis that children will carry out their interactions with the people, places and things that surround them.
Communi-cation – Mana reo	enhance their ability to effectively communicate ideas and information and solve problems; an ability to be creative and expressive through a variety of activities	Children will come to know their Māori world and the past, present and future through their ancestral language. This strand makes clear the importance of the Māori language.

Table 6.1 Continued

Curriculum strands	Learning outcomes. Children will:	Outcomes from a Māori perspective
Contribu-tion – Mana tangata	taking increasing responsibility for their own learning and care; contributing their own special strengths and interests	The importance of whānau (the extended family) is key to this strand. Children will deepen their understanding of their kinship ties to their relatives, elders and tribal origins, including the main figures in the Māori creation stories. These relationships provide the basis on which they contribute and interact to the people, places and things that surround them.

Key points

1. The principle of empowerment in Te Whāriki is 'the early childhood curriculum empowers the child to learn and grow'.
2. Four aspects of educational design that enable children to initiate learning projects are:
   – opportunities to work collaboratively with others;
   – availability of space, time and material props to develop complex pretend play scripts;
   – relationships with teachers who make an effort to get to know children and their families;
   – teachers who view children as competent learners, able to take responsibility.
3. Children are positioned with, or construct, agency in particular contexts, and may begin to recognise or construct these opportunities in other places: to assume the lead, or to take responsibility. Te Whāriki implies that even when children are in charge of their own agenda, they will be expected to watch out for the agency of others as well and mutual caring.

Reflective questions

■ What reading about children as leaders has influenced you? And, having read it, what difference did it make to your thinking?

■ Read Figure 6.1 (The act of a rascal) again. Did something capture your interest in this? What opportunities can you imagine providing for children to express different ideas and opinions from their teachers?

■ Thinking about the case study. In the early childhood centre you know best:

 – What opportunities are there for constructing a culture in the centre that is characterised by responsibility, reciprocity, mutual respect and hospitality?

 – Are cultural priorities for the families recognised and acknowledged? What rituals of mutual respect and hospitality are regular events?

 – How are the home languages of the children recognised and acknowledged? How do they have a place here?

 – Are there ways in which families (in the widest sense) are welcomed when the child begins to attend? How are relationships established and maintained?

 – What opportunities are there for collaborative work?

Note

1. This quote is included in a chapter on agency and dialogue in Carr and Lee (2012).

References

Carr, M. and Lee, W. (2012) *Learning Stories: Constructing Learner Identities in Early Education.* London: Sage.

Carr, M., Smith, A. B., Duncan, J., Jones, C., Lee, W. and Marshall, K. (2010) *Learning in the Making: Disposition and Design in Early Education.* Rotterdam: Sense.

Clark, A. and Moss, P. (2011) *Listening to Young Children: The Mosaic Approach* (2nd edn) London: NBC.

Claxton, G. (2002) *Building Learning Power: Helping Young People Become Better Learners.* Bristol: TLO Ltd.

Claxton, G., Chambers, M., Powell, G. and Lucas, B. (2011) *The Learning Powered School: A Blueprint for 21st Century Education.* Bristol: TLO Ltd.

Csikszentmihalyi, M. (1996) *Creativity: Flow and the Psychology of Discovery and Invention.* New York: HarperCollins.

Kramsch, C. (1993) *Context and Culture in Language Teaching.* Oxford: Oxford University Press.

New Zealand Ministry of Education (2009) *Te Whatu Pōkeka: Kaupapa Māori Assessment for Learning.* Wellington: Learning Media.

Smith, A. B., Taylor, N. J. and Gollop, M. M. (eds), (2000) *Children's Voices: Research, Policy and Practice.* Auckland: Longman.

Soutar, B. and Te Whānau o Mana Tamariki (2010) Growing raukura. In A. Meade (ed.), (2010) *Dispersing the Waves: Innovation in Early Childhood Education* (pp.35–40). Wellington: NZCER Press.

7 Principle four: Whānau tangata/family and community

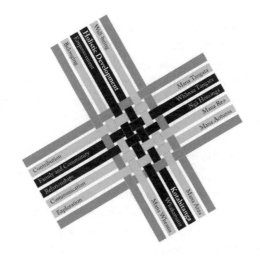

There is a great whakataukī from Kūkupa Tirakatene that has been part of our centre's life for the past few years:

E kore e taea e te whenu ki te raranga i te whāriki kia mohio tatou kia tatou.

Ma te mahi tahi o nga whenu, ma te mahi tahi o nga kairaranga, ka oti tenei whāriki.

The whāriki of our sustenance and well-being cannot be woven by one strand alone.

Only by the working together of strands and the working together of us all, will such a whāriki be completed (Teacher reflection, Jacqui).

The final principle in Te Whāriki to be discussed here is whānau tangata/ family and community. The annotation (p.42) says: 'The wider world of family and community is an integral part of the early childhood curriculum'. This refers to the responsive and reciprocal relationships with widening communities: the home and other communities to which the family belong: whānau, iwi, work, church and so on. Te Whāriki notes (p.42) that

> New Zealand is the home of Māori language and culture: curriculum in early childhood settings should promote te reo and nga tikanga Māori, making them visible and affirming their value for children from all cultural backgrounds. Adults working with children should demonstrate an understanding of the different iwi and the meaning of whānau and whānaungatanga. They should also respect the aspirations of parents and families (Te Whāriki, p.42).

As in the previous three chapters, illustrative outcomes for this principle are gathered together in Table 7.1. Recent research and writing on whānaungatanga as it is reflected in early childhood education provision (Ritchie and Rau, 2006, 2010) has further informed the implementation of Te Whāriki. Here is a quote from Marianne, who also opened the discussion in Chapter 4:

> We have given a lot of thought to the concept of Whānaungatanga, which we have come to recognise as the 'heart of relationships' (Ritchie, 1992). Valuing the importance of children's family, culture, knowledge and community, we reflected on how we support this concept to foster and enhance children's learning and well-being. And what more we could do. We created a 'Whānaungatanga board' to make visible and promote the sharing of stories from home, and we discovered that sharing promotes sharing!
>
> Another aspect of Whānaungatanga we have introduced is making connections to our family through a *mihimihi*. Children are offered the opportunity to learn and share their mihimihi, introducing themselves and their families (Marianne).

Diversity of family and community

When Te Whāriki was published the document commented on diversity across the community:

> Different cultures have different child-rearing patterns, beliefs, and traditions and may place value on different knowledge, skills and attitudes. Culturally appro-

priate ways of communicating should be fostered, and participation in the early childhood education programme by whānau, parents, extended family, and elders in the community should be encouraged (Te Whāriki p. 42).

In the second decade of the twenty-first century, the cultural picture has become immensely more diverse. A longitudinal study of 6846 children born between April 2009 and March 2010 in two regions in the north of the North Island of Aotearoa New Zealand (south Auckland and the Waikato region), *Growing Up in New Zealand,* has provided us with some information about the families and the families' communities of those born 13–14 years after the publication of Te Whāriki (Morton *et al.*, 2010). This cohort is broadly generalisable to all New Zealand children, and the 2010 description of the families before the children were born reports that one in three of them would have at least one parent who was not born in New Zealand; 20 per cent of the households do not use English as their primary language for everyday conversations at home, and one in three of the homes includes at least one parent who is multilingual. Many of the families are highly mobile, with over half having moved twice or more in the 5 years before the antenatal interview (Morton *et al.*, 2010).

The wider worlds of the families stretch over the globe. In the *Learning in the Making* study the father of 4-year-old Yasin had this to say:

> We are becoming a global village nowadays. I was just reading, banking jobs, the first qualification is a foreign language – nothing else. We feel very strongly that twenty years down the line, in the year 2025, when these children are in the workforce, at that time there will be a predominance of people who will be speaking Mandarin, obviously, because China's got a large population (Carr *et al.*, 2010 p.172).

Languages were highly valued in Yasin's home. His family immigrated to New Zealand when he was a baby and at home they spoke both English and Gujarati. Yasin's older brother had been to the same kindergarten as Yasin and the teachers knew the family well. At kindergarten Yasin seized many opportunities to talk about his family and his grandmother in India, and the teachers responded with interest. We followed up Yasin at school, and later commented:

> Yasin's conversations with teachers at the kindergarten set out the contexts of a cultural self: the country outside New Zealand, India, where his nana and extended family live, and his family in New Zealand who are widening his

perceptions of self as a global citizen by introducing him to new languages . . . By school, however, this cultural self has been left behind (p.192).

It is unusual for a national curriculum to nail its colours to the mast or, in this context, to commit to a theoretical position that includes the wider community, as Te Whāriki does with its page on Urie Bronfenbrenner's ecological system, described in Chapter 2. Bronfenbrenner was very interested in the effect of unemployment in the 1930s on families and children: the repercussions of being a child living in poverty, with reduced access to health services, poorly heated homes and unhappy parents. Research has indicated that parental aspirations for their children are a key factor in children's achievement at school (Siraj-Blatchford, 2010; Hattie, 2009); social contexts and early childhood provision outside the home influence these aspirations, as we will see in Chapter 8's discussion of ECE assessment practices.

Pierre Bourdieu's ideas are relevant here, too. Liz Brooker has written about family values and the value of families in her study of the cultural implications when the young children she researched started school. She writes about the influence of the families' expectations for the future (2002, p.39). Bourdieu's notion of 'habitus' as systems of durable dispositions that inscribe 'things to do or not to do, things to say or not to say, in relation to a "probable" upcoming future' (Bourdieu, 1990, p.53) is helpful for thinking about families' aspirations for the future, and the concept is made very accessible in Brooker's discussions. She also points out that different experiences of expectation help to structure, and perhaps to change, children's dispositions about a probable upcoming future.

We are reminded of it when we re-read Tilly Reedy, one of the architects of Te Whāriki, in an often quoted chapter based on a presentation at the 1995 Aotearoa New Zealand Early Childhood Convention. She reminds the audience that the notion of cultural transmission is central to a national curriculum:

It encourages the transmission of my cultural values, my language and tikanga, and your cultural values, your language and customs. It validates my belief systems and your belief systems . . . In all of this, Te Whāriki also recognises the child as a living link to the past, the embodiment of the present, and the hope for the future' (2003, p.74).

In the same study as that of Yasin and his family, comments by Ofeina's mother, who had migrated to New Zealand as a teenager, are relevant here:

Ofeina's mother was the fifth of seven children and when she left school she held down two jobs at the same time for a number of years, even after Ofeina and her brother were born. She talked about her ambitions for Ofeina and her brother: 'I told them, you go to University 'cos I didn't, I know I should have, but I didn't' (Carr *et al.*, 2010, p.63).

When Ofeina started at kindergarten she joined the younger children's afternoon session; families were welcome. Ofeina enjoyed spending time in the jigsaw area, where many of the mothers, aunties and grand-mothers stayed for a while to watch their children and to chat, some of them talking in Tongan, the home language of Ofeina's grandmother, who looked after her while her mother was at work. On the second afternoon of our observations we counted 17 family members early in the session: five chatting together on couches beside the jigsaw area, four on the floor helping children to do jigsaws, one at a play dough table, one standing watching, one in the children's family or office corner, two sitting outside talking and one talking to a child outside. Half an hour later there were still 14 family members there. By then two were in the kitchen, making cups of tea and cutting up fruit for the children. Early childhood settings are powerful sites: they can model for children and families, and immerse children in an environment of respect for and connections to community. Here is a comment from a parent in a kindergarten that was developing as an integrated services community centre:

This is classed as a low-decile [low socioeconomic] area and I don't think this kindergarten reflects anything like that. These teachers don't put that kind of image forward around here (Clarkin-Phillips and Carr, 2009, p.14).

Community as part of the playground

Teachers have many stories about links with community beyond the early childhood centre. They include Aotearoa New Zealand 'Bush' pro-grammes, where children regularly experience wilder places for explora-tion and challenge. These programmes have been inspired by the Danish Forest School approach (Williams-Siegfredsen, 2012) (see Figure 7.1).

At Roskill South Kindergarten, a case study described in Chapter 8, the teachers always documented visits to places like the zoo, museums and art galleries, often using a video camera and making a DVD of the trip for

Courage

Another wonderful day at Bush Kindergarten was in full swing and Urwah had been busy working with his friends. We were exploring near the commando ropes and I suggested Urwah may like to have a go on the ropes. Urwah thought for a moment and replied,"I am scared."

This began a conversation. Urwah and I talked about how it is okay to feel scared, but by participating in the task it supports your learning and fosters your disposition to persist with challenges.

Urwah took up the challenge and headed to the commando rope. After Urwah's first go it became clear Urwah had BIG plans. Urwah's aim was to walk along the entire length of the commando ropes and he was very keen to reach the next tree.

On Urwah's first attempt he made it half way along the ropes.

The commando ropes are very wobbly and Urwah experimented with how to move along the rope and also keep his body balanced.

Urwah kept trying and trying and trying. Each attempt saw Urwah gaining progress and he was getting closer and closer to the tree.

Urwah had just begun another attempt and there was a sense of anticipation in the air as Urwah was moving closer and closer to the tree.As Urwah was making progress along the rope his smile was spreading further and further across his face. Then, success! Urwah was at the end! Urwah announced, "I did it!"

"Yes indeed you did do it Urwah. Your perseverance and attitude to give it a go certainly supported you to achieve your goal!" I replied. Upon landing on the ground Urwah jumped up and down and punched the air, in total satisfaction!

What learning do I think is happening for Urwah?

Bush Kindergarten is providing another learning environment filled with opportunities and possibilities and Urwah is certainly making great plans for his time at kindergarten. Exploring in the outdoors is part of the Kiwi way of life, we are surrounded by many lovely regional parks, wilderness areas and mountains. New Zealand's outdoor environment provides many exciting possibilities for Urwah and Bush Kindergarten is providing a taste of this experience. Urwah's courage to share his fear initiated a very powerful conversation. Urwah reflected on our discussion and then chose to 'have a go'. This is a powerful mindset that will support Urwah's learning journey throughout his early childhood years and beyond. Challenges foster our disposition to persist, and Urwah's attitude to participate certainly deepened his disposition to persevere. Urwah was so proud of his achievement and celebrated in true style. Learning dispositions are robust and will support Urwah as he explores new and familiar experiences at kindergarten and home.

It was so exciting to be part of Urwah's learning today and I look forward to working alongside Urwah as he continues to make plans for his time at Bush Kindergarten.

Figure 7.1 Courage

Written by Karen

each child's portfolio, so that the experience can be revisited at home and with groups of children at the centre. Photographs are taken, too, and children invited to make comments on them for a book to be made. An example of this is included in Book 1 (p.17) of the teacher resource, *Kei Tua o Te Pae. Assessment for Learning: Early Childhood Exemplars*. The children went on a trip to a 'weird and wonderful' exhibition at the local museum. The teachers asked the children for their assessments of the trip together with photographs of them at the museum, and these were included in a book. The comments illustrated that the children found very different things interesting in what was apparently the same experience for them all:

> George: My name is George. I am wearing my dragon shirt. The bees were going outside. I liked the crabs. I liked it when the bees went outside. I sat next to my mum on the bus.
>
> Rachael: When I got on the bus I was scared. My dad put on his sunglasses. I sat on the bus. I saw Jane on the bus. She had her butterfly wings on. Fuka's dad was driving the bus.
>
> Teyilati: I liked the spiders in a glass cage. They were big. I liked looking at the spiders. I played in the sandpit. There were toys to play with.

Documenting the values

One of the important aspects of a national curriculum is that it is a *document*; it reifies the philosophy (makes it material, turns it into an object). It can include a poster for the wall, and the first distribution of the Te Whāriki document to early childhood centres included the framework in Chapter 2, together with all the indicative outcomes. Teachers and families can revisit the big picture, to keep in mind the values that under-pin the planning for teaching pathways and learning journeys. A curriculum document can take us beyond daily 'how to' questions, the day-to-day pedagogy, to remind us of the bigger 'what' questions. This is what Jo does in Figure 7.2 (My thoughts) where she describes a possible self for Sam as a curious adventurer.

A curriculum on its own is not sufficient, however, and the next two chapters in this book outline further supports that add a dynamic and accountable dimension to a curriculum statement: the documentation of children's learning that teachers, families and children can revisit; and professional development.

My thoughts . . .

My moments with Sam today reminded me of the importance of stopping, slowing down, watching and really listening. It was in doing this that I was able to see and be a part of Sam's engagement with his environment and then his interaction with me. And what a special moment to treasure.

Sam showed a burning curiosity in the world around him. Wherever his attention was directed he connected, giving it his all. He was captivating, when he engaged with me, drawing me in to his communication, making sure that I was interested and involved.This eagerness to explore and make connections with people and things will serve him well as he makes the choices about where his interests lead his learning.

I wanted to write this story for Sam today because I want Sam to see (when he revisits his learning journey in the years to come) that when he was four months old he was an explorer, finding his place in the great outdoors. He was an adventurer who was eager to meet new people and build relationships and I wanted Sam to know that I thought WOW Sam, we are going to have some fun times here with you at Emmett Street.

Figure 7.2 My thoughts

Written by Jo

A case study: Wilton Playcentre

Background

Wilton Playcentre was a designated Centre of Innovation from 2003 to 2006 (see Wilton Playcentre *et al.*, 2005). The playcentre is located in Wilton, a suburb in Wellington, the capital city of Aotearoa New Zealand. It was founded in the late 1950s and operates in a former church building. The playcentre is sessional, with 16–20 children from birth to the age of 6 years attending in mixed age groups for 1, 2, 3 or 4 sessions a week. While a child is under 2.5 years old a parent or caregiver attends the session with them. Required ratios are 1:5 for children over 2.5 years old. These are playcentre requirements and the ratios are higher than regulated staff ratios in other centres.

Mana whenua – belonging. Parents work as a collective

The playcentre philosophy is underpinned by a belief that families are the prime educators of their children. Parent volunteers work as a collective to take responsibility for management and the education programme—the educators working with children are mothers and fathers of the children enrolled. At Wilton Playcentre, a minimum commitment is participation in one duty session per week, unless parents are on maternity leave. Each session is run by a team of five or six parents/educators who are responsible for the same session each week.

Mana atua – well-being. A culture of supportive relationships

The key features that support wellbeing and connectedness are a common purpose built around children, a culture of supportive relationships, opportunities for families and children to learn together, opportunities for families and children to contribute understanding and expertise, participation of parents in curriculum, assessment and planning. These can be present in teacher-led services too.

Mana aotūroa – exploration

Parents are learners too. Most parents have undertaken training courses run by the Playcentre Association. These cover areas such as child development, play and learning, parenting skills, planning and delivery of programmes, Te Whāriki, facilitation skills and management skills. In every session, two or three parents hold higher levels of training so that collectively there is a pool of expertise. During the Centre of Innovation research, parents made observations and analysed their interactions with children using a quality rating scale developed for Aotearoa New Zealand contexts. They had then discussed the ratings as a collective, and decided on two areas they wanted to work on. One was to try to extend children's thinking by asking open-ended questions that encourage children to choose their own answers and to engage in sustained shared thinking.

Mana reo – communication. A print-saturated environment

The second area was to provide a 'print saturated environment' that encouraged print awareness and exploration of thoughts, experiences and ideas using symbols. A workshop was held with parents so they were confident about these focus areas. Map making and letter writing became undertakings that captured children's interest:

Nyah is aged 3 years and 10 months. Martha is Nyah's mother and Bronwyn is another playcentre adult. Open-ended questions helped Nyah to start thinking more deeply and when she is given time to respond she comes up with a creative, considered idea. Nyah's ongoing fascination with place relationships and maps [noticed by Martha at home and adults at the playcentre when they analysed her learning stories] is evident. Arguably, she has lifted her thinking to a higher level, understanding maps in abstract thought, not as a piece of paper. Nyah is responding to a letter from Elliot, a playcentre child, who was overseas for 3 months.

Nyah: I am going to write a letter to Elliot.

Martha (to Bronwyn): We received a letter from Elliot last term. He and his family are in America.

Bronwyn: How did Elliot's letter get to us?

Nyah: He put it in the letter box.

Martha: And then what happened? . . . How do you think the letter got from the letterbox Elliot put it in to our letterbox?

Nyah: The mailman came and got it.

Martha: There is lots of water and sea between America and New Zealand. How do you think the letter got here?

Nyah: Well the mailman picked up the letter from the mailbox and came on a boat to us and then put the letter into our mailbox here at playcentre.

[Martha: After I wrote this I checked with Nyah that it was right. She said that it was right but also thinks that the mailman ties his boat up here in Wellington before delivering the letter to playcentre.]

Martha: Then what does he do?

Nyah: He goes back.
Martha: To where the letter came from?
Nyah: Yeah!

The impetus for the letter writing came from the children but the adults extended it – making a post box captured the interest of many children and once one was made, it further encouraged children to write letters.

Mana tangata – contribution. Decisions are made by consensus

All decisions are made by consensus. The playcentre's values and educational practice are based on the aspirations for children and the four principles of Te Whāriki. Playcentre parents regard these as equally applicable to parents and children. For the Centre of Innovation programme the playcentre offered itself as a case study of ways in which playcentre children, parents and whānau (extended family) work together as a community of learners. The playcentre's definition of 'community of learners' drew on Rogoff's (1994) idea that people learn through their interactions with others by participating in shared endeavours. This contrasts with pedagogy that is largely adult-directed or child-led. The curriculum is built using children's ideas as entry points for negotiating activities and topics. The community of learners at Wilton Playcentre is mainly parents and children working together.

Some illustrative outcomes from Te Whāriki for this curriculum principle

Table 7.1 provides examples taken from Te Whāriki explanations of whānau tangata/family and community and the indicative outcomes from the strands.

Table 7.1 Whānau tangata/family and community

Curriculum strands	Learning outcomes. Children develop:
Belonging – Mana whenua	an understanding of the links between the early childhood education setting and the known and familiar wider world;
	an interest and pleasure in discovering an unfamiliar wider world;
	connecting links between the early childhood education setting and other settings that relate to the child, such as home, school or a parent's workplace;

Table 7.1 Continued

Curriculum strands	Learning outcomes. Children develop:
	knowledge about the role of the wider world of work, such as the hospital, the supermarket or the fire service;
	an understanding that routines, customs and events can be different in other settings.
Well-being – Mana atua	trust that the local communities' spiritual dimensions of health and well-being are recognised in practice;
	respect for rules about not harming others and the environment and an understanding of the reasons for such rules.
Exploration – Mana aotūroa	familiarity with stories from different cultures about the living world, including myths and legends and oral, non-fictional and fictional forms;
	a knowledge of features of the land that are of local significance, such as the local river or mountain;
	respect and a developing sense of responsibility for the well-being of both the living and the non-living environment;
Communication – Mana reo	Confidence that their first language is valued;
	familiarity with an appropriate selection of the stories and literature valued by the cultures in the community;
	an increasing familiarity with a selection of the art, craft, songs, music, and stories that are valued by the cultures in the community;
	an appreciation of te reo as a living and relevant language.
Contribution – Mana tangata	confidence that their family background is viewed positively in the early childhood education setting;
	a sense of responsibility and respect for the needs and well-being of the group;
	an appreciation of the ways in which they can make contributions to groups and to group well-being.

Key points

1. The principle of family and community in Te Whāriki is 'The wider world of family and community is an integral part of the early childhood curriculum'. An emphasis on early childhood services assisting children and their families to 'access the resources necessary to enable them to direct their own lives'.

2. In the Te Whāriki approach, culturally appropriate ways of communicating are fostered and participation in the early childhood education programme by whānau, parents, extended family and elders in the community are encouraged.
3. The families in each early childhood centre can represent a wide range of home languages and cultures.
4. Families develop systems of durable dispositions that inscribe 'things to do or not to do, things to say or not to say, in relation to a "probable" upcoming future'. Pierre Bourdieu's ideas are relevant to early childhood curriculum discussions.
5. Parental aspirations are identified as influential factors in children's achievement at school.
6. The wider community is part of the playground: the bush (in Aotearoa New Zealand and Australia), zoo, museum and art gallery.
7. A curriculum document reifies learning values and outcomes: they become a thing or a material object. The values and outcomes are written down and can be revisited and talked about together, reminding us of the big 'what' questions of early childhood education. Documented assessments do this, too.

Reflective questions

- Jacqui introduces this chapter with a whakataukī. Do you have a favourite proverb, metaphor, poem, song or saying that reflects some of the ideas about learning and teaching that you love?
- Tilly Reedy said 'Te Whāriki also recognises the child as a living link to the past, the embodiment of the present, and the hope for the future'. How might these aspects of a child's identity be included in early childhood provision?
- What reading about families and family relationships has influenced you? And, having read it, what difference did it make to your thinking?
- Read Figure 7.1 (Courage) again. Did something capture your interest in this?
- Read Figure 7.2 (My thoughts) again. What do you think the family response would be to reading this story about Sam at 4 months old?
- Thinking about the case study. In the early childhood centre you know best:
  - In what way are parents enabled to be teachers here?
  - In what way are parents enabled to be learners here?

- Are there examples of families being supported when they need assistance? What makes this possible? What makes it difficult? How could this be improved? What steps might you be able to take to improve the opportunities for this centre to be a supportive community?
- What early literacies are available?
- Are there ways in which families are able to be part of the decision-making here? Are there enough ways? Reflect on your image of the families as contributors of their cultural capital and passionate about a good life for their children.

References

Bourdieu, P. (1990) *The Logic of Practice*. Trans. R. Nice. Cambridge: Polity.

Brooker, L. (2002) *Starting School: Young Children Learning Cultures*. Buckingham: Open University Press.

Clarkin-Phillips, J. and Carr, M. (2009) Strengthening responsive and reciprocal relationships in a whānau tangata centre. *Early Childhood Folio*, 13, 12–15.

Morton, S. M. B., Atatoa Carr, P. E., Bandara D. K. *et al.* (2010) *Growing Up in New Zealand: A Longitudinal Study of New Zealand Children and Their Families. Report 1: Before We Are Born*. Auckland: University of Auckland.

Ritchie, J. and Rau, C. (2006) Whakawhānaungatanga partnerships for bi-cultural development in early childhood education and care. *Teaching and Learning Research Initiative Final Report*. Retrieved 18 January 2012 from http://www.tlri.org.nz/whakawhānaungatanga%E2%80%94partnerships-bicultural-development-early-childhood-care-and-education/.

Ritchie, J. and Rau, C. (2010) Poipoia te Tamaiti kia tū tangata, The first years – ngā tau tuatahi. *New Zealand Journal of Infant and Toddler Education*, 12(1), 16–22.

Rogoff, B. (1994) Developing understanding of the idea of community of learners. *Mind, Culture, and Activity*, 1(4), 209–28.

Siraj-Blatchford, I. (2010) Learning in the home and at school: how working class children 'succeed against the odds'. *British Educational Research Journal*, 36(3), 463–82.

Williams-Siegfredsen, J. (2012) *Understanding the Danish Forest School Approach: Early Years Education in Practice*. London: Routledge.

Wilton Playcentre members, with Pam Cubey and Linda Mitchell (2005) Innovation at Wilton Playcentre. In A. Meade (ed.) *Catching the Waves: Innovation in Early Childhood Education* (pp.45–53). Wellington: NZCER Press.

8 Weaving: documentation, assessment and planning

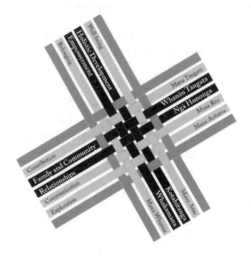

From Australia Trish Tranfa writes:

> The influence of the New Zealand Learning Story philosophy has provided us with a much needed strategy for articulating children's learning in a way that is meaningful for children and their families. This narrative form of assessment enables us to share our beliefs, values and connections with children and to make connections with curriculum frameworks and theories about learning. When educators share learning stories with each other they are challenged to consider their practices more deeply and are motivated to seek new ways of understanding and articulating teaching and learning processes.

Each of the last four chapters illustrates the ways in which the curriculum principles have been woven through each of the five strands of outcomes. In this chapter this weaving is described in three other ways:

- the interweaving of learning and teaching in the goals;
- the documentation and assessment;
- the planning practices.

The interweaving of learning and teaching in the goals as participation in a learning community

The goals in Te Whāriki emphasise children experiencing an environment that facilitates, or affords the five strands (see Figure 2.2 in Chapter 2). They describe a facilitating environment as promoting, nurturing, connecting, providing opportunity, affirming, encouraging, experiencing, valuing, recognising – all of which emphasise the Te Whāriki approach to learning and teaching, which identifies the site of learning as being in the space between the learners and the learning environment (the people, places and things). One of us had this to say in a presentation 11 years after Te Whāriki was published:

> It is interesting that we were guided by Māori advisors, for whom the word *ako* means both teaching and learning, and Lev Vygotsky had in his lexicon the Russian word *obuchenie*, which also means both teaching and learning (Carr, 2005, p.40).

The curriculum strands are about both teaching and learning. The goals mostly focus on the teaching; the outcomes focus on what the children will be learning. The pedagogy, what the adults, children and places and things do together, interweaves teaching and learning. It is the notion of learning as participation, as Barbara Rogoff (1990) and others have argued, that connects the goals and the outcomes. Competence and pedagogy are situated within the community. A chapter written in the same year that Te Whāriki was published argues that participation focuses on

> engagement that maintains the person's interpersonal relations and identity in communities in which the individual has a significant personal investment. This view emphasises how people's very identities derive from their participatory relationships in communities. According to this view students can become engaged in learning by participating in communities where learning is valued (Greeno *et al.*, 1996, p.26).

The weaving of a curriculum in documentation and assessment

From England, Nora Waugh writes:

> The links between theory and practice are clear and very accessible in Te Whāriki, leading to a much better understanding of how children learn. Learning journals now capture the magic of children as they discover the world in a way other more formal assessments could never do.

Assessment practices can prohibit, weaken, support or strengthen a curriculum. Mindful of this, a research contract and then a resource was funded by the Ministry of Education to develop assessment practices that would support and strengthen Te Whāriki. Research was initially carried out in five early childhood settings: a home-based setting, a childcare centre, a kindergarten, a playcentre and a kōhanga reo. A DVD package, including workshops, was developed from this research (Carr, 1998a, 1998b). Later, a 20-booklet resource entitled *Kei Tua o te Pae* was developed (Carr *et al.*, 2004, 2007, 2009) with exemplars of assessment practice and an accompanying text that added a theoretical and research-based commentary. These booklets, including a booklet on assessment of each of the five curriculum strands, were distributed to all early childhood centres or services and primary schools, and are made available on the New Zealand Ministry of Education website. Mary-Jane Drummond made the following comment:

> Another important alternative possibility is to be found in the work of writers and educators in New Zealand; their curriculum guidelines for early childhood, adopted in 1996, a bilingual document known as Te Whāriki, has stimulated great interest in other early years professional communities around the world . . . [The approach to assessment is] based on narrative, in which the dominant metaphor is story, not levels or goals . . . In this approach, it is apparent that the New Zealand educators have rejected the view that learning is momentary and discontinuous, convergent and normative, easily measured and quantified, a score, grade or level that children have, to varying degrees, rather than something they continuously do (Drummond, 2008, p.14).

This assessment practice has responded to the call of the four principles in *Te Whāriki* (see Carr and Lee, 2012), the demands of the five strands of teaching and learning, and the weaving together of knowledge and learning dispositions as a unit of analysis for studying learning in the early years. It was very important that the assessment processes should be consistent with the principles of Te Whāriki. For example, take the Te Whāriki principle of empowerment. The early childhood curriculum (assessment practices and processes) will empower the child to learn and grow. Implicit in this principle is the importance of documenting a 'credit' view of the child. As Egon Guba and Yvonna Lincoln argue, a curriculum that is reciprocal, interacting and empowering should be assessed or evaluated by processes that are also reciprocal, interacting and empowering. They also make the comment that many assessment procedures imply that 'what cannot be measured cannot be real' (1989, p.37). In the case of Te Whāriki, this would include aims and outcomes such as respect, curiosity, trust, reflection, belonging, confidence and responsibility.

These assessments are written as stories of learning in familiar contexts. The learning story is first and foremost a story written to the child and the family, recognising the complex nature of learning involving affective, social and motivational implications. The assessment practice of learning stories acknowledges assessment as a powerful force for learning. There are three key elements of a learning story:

- the narrative that describes the significant learning event
- the analysis of the learning, which can be described as asking the question, 'What have I learnt about Jack today?' or 'what learning do I think was happening?'
- the planning. This is not written for every story but may be listed as 'opportunities and possibilities'.

Figure 8.1, Kellen's love for bracelets, exemplifies these three aspects. Learning stories are gathered together in a portfolio, file or profile book. They can be read as a number of 'chains of episodes' (Carr and Lee, 2012), describing progress and continuity.

Examples of the uses and values of learning stories

1. Enhancing children's sense of themselves as capable people and competent learners; a learning story may:

Kellen's love for bracelets

Last week Kellen came to kindergarten wearing several silver bracelets. He told me they were his mummy's. For the next two days Kellen proudly wore the bracelets and then he discovered the threading beads. Threading has been part of Roskill South Kindergarten's programme for over a year now and during this time many children have created some wonderful jewellery.

Kellen chose the beads and began to create his own bracelet. Concentrating and carefully threading beads onto the coloured string, Kellen's bracelet began to grow. When he had finished threading, Kellen came to me and I tied his bracelet around his wrist.

The next day, Kylie, Kellen's mum, told me that Kellen had not taken his bracelet off and for the next week it could be seen being worn around his wrist. Since creating his first bracelet, Kellen has spent many happy afternoons creating more.

What Learning Do I Think Is Happening?

Threading is an activity that provides the opportunity for pre-maths skills, involving patterning, colours, counting and hand-eye co-ordination.

Possibilities

We will continue to keep the threading area well stocked and provide provocation with photos and books on threading.

Kellen, you might like to create a necklace for your mummy, or maybe some bracelets. I wonder if you would like to look at the books we have that show different patterns for bracelets. Maybe you could create your own patterns.

Kellen set a goal for himself today and showed persistence and determination as he threaded small and large beads onto his string to create his bracelet. At Roskill South we encourage the children to be capable and competent learners, making their own choices and directing their own learning. Kellen is developing these skills and is taking the opportunity to make plans and direct his own learning.

Figure 8.1 Kellen's love for bracelets

Written by Kim

- focus on children's developing identities as learners, based on the learning dispositions that parallel the five strands of the curriculum; and make visible the knowledge and skills of the learner
- take a credit rather than a deficit approach, in order to develop learning repertoires, working theories and dispositions
- include children's voices
- describe progress in a way that families and children can appreciate.

Learning stories should show how children enhance their sense of themselves as capable people and competent learners. Learning stories are about children's developing identities as learners, based on the learning dispositions that parallel the five strands of the Te Whāriki curriculum (that is, the tips of the curriculum iceberg).

Being a learner includes a view of the self as interested and interesting; someone who gets involved; a learner who persists with difficulty and uncertainty; a communicator; and a citizen or member of a community, with rights and responsibilities (Carr, 2001).

2. Reflecting the holistic way in which children learn, a learning story may:
   - follow children's enterprises over several days
   - document centre and community projects
   - document daily routines in a way that illuminates them as meaningful, child-centred learning experiences
   - focus on children solving problems and persisting with difficulty, as well as the outcome of the project being explored.

Holding a view of the importance of holistic development will ensure that the holistic nature of the curriculum encourages and supports teachers to document meaningful experiences and relationships. As Diti Hill (2001) states: 'children do not live their lives in curriculum fragments'. Creating a curriculum that acknowledges this principle will enable children to engage in the setting as curious and engaged explorers, able to engage in sustained projects over time, supported by listening and reflective practitioners.

3. To reflect the reciprocal relationships between the child, people and the learning environment, a learning story may:
   - advocate early childhood
   - reflect the relationship with the environment
   - reflect the relationship with the teacher
   - illuminate the opportunities available to children to take increasing responsibility for their safety, health, learning and each other.

In ensuring the assessment is consistent with the aims of a reciprocal and responsive curriculum, narrative assessment will give practitioners an opportunity to strongly reflect the wider picture of relationships in the learning environment.

4. By involving parents/guardians and, where appropriate, whānau, a learning story may:
   - be accessible and interesting to families
   - make visible the funds of knowledge that children bring with them into the early childhood setting
   - make visible and value the everyday connections with family and whānau through conversation and familiar events and objects
   - reflect the care moments and interactions that affirm the infant or child's cultural and family identity.

Learning stories advocate the importance of including families as part of assessment practices and processes and provide pathways for their involvement. What is written may have a powerful impact on the family and on the family's view of their child. Documentation that illuminates a child's interests, passions and strengths are intended to make an important contribution not only to the child's sense of self but also to the parents' expectations of the child and, ultimately, the identity of the child as a learner.

Planning with the weaving in mind

Planning is a third way in which the curriculum is woven. As learning stories became more embedded in the culture of early childhood settings, it became increasingly obvious that a different process for planning was critical. The notions of noticing, recognising and responding became the key to effectiveness in planning. Teachers were now responding in a more intuitive manner. Old methods of planning were often around topics driven by teachers: topics that may or may not have been of interest to the children. Using a Te Whāriki lens and a view of curriculum as being co-constructed between teachers or educators and children meant that children's interests and passions were the key focus of programme development. These processes also encourage and support teachers and educators and families to initiate programme possibilities. Given that planning needed to be directed towards individuals as well as groups, and to articulate learning as well as experiences, a multi-level approach was called for. Programme planning in early childhood settings began to develop in the following ways:

Planning for an individual child's learning that concerns that child alone and is based on learning stories or other approaches to individual assessment, recorded and unrecorded

As teachers observe children's interests and passions they encourage the children to be self-directed learners who are setting their own goals for learning. It is the 'opportunities and possibilities' section in learning stories that engages planning aspects. We needed to be mindful that this aspect of planning must be left open in order to enable responsiveness to children's learning.

'Progress' is difficult to define, and the Te Whāriki approach had moved away from some of the stages of development that we used to rely on. In some contexts, assessment for learning assumes that we know what the next step should be, but for complex learning we do not always know. Because learning is more effective when educational activities are meaningful and relevant to children, and because assessment should be in familiar contexts, the teacher

> always has to be responsive to the students' goals, as these emerge in the course of activity, and by collaborating with them in the achievement of their individual goals, to enable them to extend their mastery and at the same time their potential for further development. From a teacher's perspective, therefore, one is always aiming at a moving target (Wells, 1999, pp.318–19).

Examples of planning in this case include making a conscious effort to draw on children's leadership or motivational skills, providing them with the opportunity to practise their skills and encouraging them to extend their persistence into another context. The parent and child will also contribute to planning here. For example, a teacher might write, 'I will ask Jessica what she would like to do next so that she can decide on her future goals'.

Planning that is inspired by children's interest in something

'This will be in an area that the teachers think will enthuse others, and which has the potential to extend children's thinking and problem-solving and to take children's knowledge and dispositions to new heights. This planning is often displayed publicly and often uses the metaphor of planning as work that is like a ripple in a pond. A core idea leads off on a tangent over time as children's and educators' thoughts are discussed, shared and documented. Think of this as research or an investigation. This suggests the notion of children and teachers collaborating and learning about something they are interested in and with which they are unfamiliar.

Planning that is inspired by teachers and educators who bring their own professional knowledge around pedagogically sound practice and what is important, given the society and community in which we live

This strand of planning may also be driven by a teacher's passion. This might be a focus that arises from a review of a strand of Te Whāriki: for example, a recognition that you could be doing more in the way of providing equitable opportunities for learning, irrespective of gender, ability, age, ethnicity or background. It might also be something that is suggested as a result of professional learning, for example, increasing the focus on the arts or literacy.

Planning that is publicly displayed is more interesting when it is a growing, living record, rather than a static display

Inclusion of photos and examples of children's work, ideas, questions or thoughts as well as teachers' reflections makes visible the link between documentation and practice. It also contributes to evaluation by developing a public display that invites contributions from children, parents and teachers. Planning will be more dynamic and responsive to the children in the centre. Much of the planning now looks like a process of retrospective exploration – a looking back and a pulling together of the actual events and responses of all participants to children's learning. Teachers and educators use reflective questions to draw out and make visible their intentions and the intentions of children around planning. This stimulates further reflective thinking and writing. Some examples of the kinds of questions they might ask themselves are set out at the end of this chapter.

What follows is a small window into a story of interest (a planning story) written by the teachers of Roskill South Kindergarten. It was in this centre that the first planning stories were written. Subsequently, many settings are developing their own planning stories that tell in depth the stories of learning that are happening in their contexts. The threading story in Figure 8.2 came from a story that is some 82 slides in total. The story was written retrospectively by the teaching team, pulling together the work they had already documented over a 2-year period around this area of interest: 'threading'. The teachers raised many of the questions outlined above, as they reflected on their learning story documentation and brought together what they felt were the significant features of this work.

Threading story

Roskill South Kindergarten

Teachers at Roskill South: Karen, Kate and Kim. Other relieving teachers who contributed during this period were: Jacqui, Anita and Jane

Figure 8.2 Threading story

The story begins . . .

Threading thrill

The interest began when the children were playing a game of matching the dice to caterpillar beads. To make the caterpillar they had to string the corresponding coloured bead to the dice. As many children were involved, Jane introduced the threading kit to the group so everyone would get a turn. Following on from that, the following Monday we put the same threading kit out when a few children said they wanted to make necklaces so they could take them home. So I gathered a few items and string.

Some amazing things started to happen . . .

Throughout the week, children came back many times to make bracelets and necklaces for themselves and family members. The straws appeared easier to thread on cotton but if you did not hold it tightly you could lose your whole creation. The problem-solving was a continual process. The children gathered in small groups and chatted with each other about things that were going on at kindergarten and home. It was great for us as we learnt a lot about the children. To start with they had to decide what length of cotton they wanted and then proceed to cut it. Sometimes it was too short to go around their head

and it turned into a bracelet so they made another one that would fit around their neck. At times the process was a long one. We started to notice that children were making random patterns and some children were very selective in their designs.

Felt squares and resources provide provocation – Jacqui reflects

Olivia's beautiful work

Today I discovered Olivia at the bead table creating another wonderful design. I knew both Kim and Kate had spent time with Olivia and photographed her as she had created her first pieces so I was very excited to see what was on the cards for today!

We had talked about how some of the necklaces we had downloaded from the Internet followed patterns, and had made pattern cards for the children to use as provocation, the intention being that these would scaffold them towards designing their own patterns.

Olivia scanned the pattern cards and began to follow one that I had created. It was not long before Olivia had completed her pattern . . .

I wondered what she would do next? . . .

'I want to make it for real now!' Olivia said. I was very excited! 'How do you think we can thread the glass stones?' I asked, not actually knowing quite how we could do it myself! Olivia tapped her finger on her chin; I could almost see the thinking happening . . .

'I don't know,' Olivia replied. Then suddenly I had an idea (well, I actually had a few, so I thought it was a great time to try them out!). 'Maybe we could try to use a very small nail and bang a hole into it?' I suggested. Olivia nodded and so off we went to trial our idea, but alas and alack, it didn't work! 'Maybe we could glue them onto a stick and then glue the stick to the cord?' I said. 'Yeah, let's try that one.' Olivia decided.

Olivia took her collection of glass beads to the glue gun area and began her experiment. I grabbed the camera and began to capture Olivia as her creation took shape.

It wasn't long before Olivia's design was really coming together. I was so glad that our idea had worked! Now it was time to add the cord. Karen had just brought some leather and I showed it to Olivia, explaining to her that it would be stronger than the fishing wire. Olivia took this on board and held up the leather, measuring the length she needed. 'I want it to be long. I want it to hang down to here,' Olivia said as she held the cord around her neck. We cut the cord to Olivia's specified length, then she took her creation back to the glue gun area and added the cord!

'I did it Jacqui. It's all done!' Olivia said with pride!

I was amazed with Olivia's necklace and so were all of her friends. There was a big buzz around Olivia's work and I wondered whether this would inspire Olivia and her friends to continue to explore their interest in jewellery making?

I didn't have to wait long to find out . . .

I set up the bead tables today with great anticipation of the girls' arrival! Olivia was first and sifted through the patterns, choosing a new challenge.

'I'm gonna make a necklace for Gracie', Olivia announced. Then she began working on her chosen pattern, a beautiful shell design! It was not long before Amelia arrived and began her beautiful necklace. Soon Olivia and Amelia were working

together; Olivia leading the way and Amelia happily taking her advice.

Olivia gave Amelia lots of encouragement and support as they sat together designing their pieces.

What learning is happening for Olivia?

Well, where do I begin? I was just absolutely amazed at Olivia's skill and ability to create such an amazing piece! We often write about the importance of our children mastering the dispositions of learning that we view with such importance and today Olivia showed that she is indeed a master of her own learning!

Olivia took an interest in the necklace making straight away and set herself goal after goal each day. As a teacher, I saw my role as one of support for Olivia because she is already an expert at directing her own learning and discovering new and exciting challenges for herself. I did, however, wonder how I could provide further provocation for Olivia and her friends so I downloaded a whole lot of images of necklaces and bead-work from the Internet for them, hoping this would add to the interest. This was a huge success and Olivia pointed out to me that she could see patterns being used in the photos. This encouraged Olivia to explore the possibilities of creating her own patterns and the word 'designing' was used to express how she was going to create her own necklace.

Olivia created a cool necklace based on a pattern she had seen early on in the day. Olivia is showing she has the ability to take information on board and give it a personal twist. Olivia then began to use trial and error to make her ideas come to life. She was very keen on using the beautiful glass shapes in her necklace but the problem was they didn't have any holes!

Olivia explained this to me and together we problem-solved until we came up with a winning answer. Then Olivia was off again, directing her own learning and explaining her work to her eager friends as she began to piece her necklace together.

Olivia worked tirelessly, never losing sight of her goal. Olivia has such a high level of persistence and I think because she has had so many successful moments at kindergarten she now expects only the best when she works, and has the ability to set and raise the bar for herself each time she takes on a new challenge. Olivia also took on the role as a leader today, helping her friend Amelia as she began her journey in necklace making. It was great to see Olivia taking up this challenge, because she works so well in a team environment and it was lovely to see her shine by taking the lead.

This necklace sparked such a buzz amongst the rest of the children, but it was almost as if Olivia was oblivious to it all. She is so industrious and I could see her main objective was to

have a finished piece to take home and share with her family. Olivia is so family orientated and this is a tribute to you and the wonderful sense of belonging and well-being that you have instilled in Olivia. My heart just melted when Olivia completed her necklace and then informed me that tomorrow she was going to create a necklace for Gracie. What a wonderful sense of commitment and love Olivia has for you guys, pure magic! When Olivia arrived and began her necklace for Gracie she worked with speed and showed just how quickly she has mastered the art of threading. It was all I could do not to cry when she saw Mum and Gracie arrive.

I grabbed the camera and captured the moment Olivia put the necklace onto Gracie, just beautiful!

What did we do?

Team reflection

We noticed, recognised and responded to children's interests and documented their learning. *Kei Tua o te Pae* (Book 1, 2004, p.6) reminds us that the difference in competence between recognising, responding and documenting is the 'application of professional expertise and judgements'. This means as teachers we are constantly reflecting on our practice and deepening this framework, as it becomes more and more a part of who we are. This is wise practice.

Learning stories support children to celebrate and revisit their learning with their friends, whānau, family and teachers. Revisiting prior learning supports children to reflect on their own learning, extend their ideas and add to the complexity of their work.

Threading provided real work

Te Whāriki reminds us:

> Children should have easy access to resources that enable them to express themselves creatively and that help them to develop concepts of mathematics, reading and writing (Te Whāriki, p.73).

Providing authentic beads inspired the children to create genuine pieces of jewellery. This was meaningful work.

The threading area provides . . . teaching team reflects

In years gone by it was expected that every child mass-produced gifts to acknowledge celebrations. We can recall the hassle of ensuring every child produced a gift, whether they wanted to or not. Since our thinking has changed and we have embraced the learning stories framework we work with the child's strengths and passions, and this means that children create what is real and authentic to them. Children choose when they would like to make a gift and what they would like to make.

What learning is happening?

There are many learning lenses that threading can be viewed through. Here are just a few:

- mulitcultural knowledges about beading (see next section)
- learning dispositions: taking an interest, being involved
- persisting with difficulty, communicating ideas, taking responsibility
- mathematical skills: patterning, perspective, sorting, classifying things, symmetry, predicting and measuring
- design and creativity
- respect for the environment
- social competence
- kindness
- fine motor development to support the early literacy journey
- hand–eye co-ordination

History of threading

Information we gathered from ezinearticles.com

The art of beading has been around nearly as long as humans have been. From the moment an ancient human found a shell or stone with a natural perforation and strung it on a piece of vine to wear around their neck, beading has been popular in one form or another. Whether those objects were worn as a religious symbol, for personal adornment or to permeate them with special powers doesn't matter. Bead stringing is the first form of beading and it persists today.

About 3000 years ago, the Egyptians learned to make glass and the next logical step was creating glass beads. They elevated the art of beading to a high level that is still admired today for its beauty and elements of design.

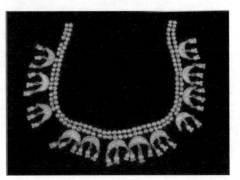

Beading was, and still is, a part of Native American Society. The process of making the quill work was sacred, but the finished piece, to be worn or used by someone, was not considered sacred. The product was of secondary importance to the process of manufacture. The focus was on the thoughts and prayers and the work, not on the finished piece – very different from Western society, which tends to value the finished product and ignores the process of creation.

There are contemporary beaders who report that beading is almost a spiritual experience for them as they embrace the art of creation as much as the finished work, the focus being on perfecting the art rather than a race to complete the final product.

It is interesting to note early thinking about the value of beading work. We can see similarities in our thinking today.

We have noticed that all children choose to work in the threading area irrespective of gender.

What surprised me? Kim reflects

When threading first started I never imagined it would become such an integral part of the programme at Roskill South. I am still amazed at the interest threading creates after this length of time. When the children first began threading they would often cut the thread too short and a necklace would become a bracelet. Now they are quite accepting of changing their design or to rethread their beads on longer thread to make their necklace. There is always a steady flow of children at the table, continually setting their own goals, making plans and

> challenging themselves to make different creations from one day to the next. Patterning and many different designs have been created. I have noticed new leaders emerge and share their passion with others. These leaders play an important part in the growth of threading. There were subtle connections evolving between patterning, colours and design between threading and mosaics.

A case study: Roskill South Kindergarten

Introduction

Roskill South Kindergarten provided the planning story (Figure 8.2) in this chapter. This kindergarten was one of the first Centres of Innovation (2003 to 2005). It is a sessional kindergarten running five morning sessions and three afternoon sessions a week, with 45 children in the morning and another 45 younger children in the afternoon. At any one time, therefore, the three degree-qualified teachers were developing relationships with 90 children and up to 90 families.

The kindergarten is set in an area of low-income housing in the largest city of Aotearoa New Zealand (Auckland, population 1.4 million) where at the beginning of the Centre of Innovation project there were 17 different home languages. One response to this demanding task was that the teachers have become very literate in information communication technology. They regularly use ICT to document the learning of individuals and groups. Children's portfolios are regularly used to revisit learning experiences and discuss learning outcomes. As well, they share their learning journeys with groups of learners, share understandings with each other, communicate with families about their children's learning and progress and dialogue about planning.

There are four digital cameras available and these are charged each day and are ready to hand; one for each of the teachers, and one for the children. The cameras are also lent to the families. A video camera is also available and each of the three teachers has a laptop. DVD recordings of trips from the kindergarten are sent home to every family. All the children's learning stories are collected together on a DVD, along with the portfolio that has travelled to and fro between kindergarten and home for the previous 18 months to 2 years, and which is finally given to each child when they leave for school.

The story of the Centre's early struggles, with minimal technology, is told in a chapter of Joce Nuttall's edited book, *Weaving Te Whāriki*. Their focus for the Centre of Innovation project was using ICT to strengthen everyday learning and teaching practices, engage families, and enhance the quality of teacher reflection and planning. Examples of practice, with this chapter's focus in mind, are explained below.

The aspiration

At Roskill South, ICT enables children to develop and hold a view of themselves as confident and competent learners by 'reading' a range of documentation and revisiting the learning. The teachers take photos and sometimes some video footage. Some of the photographs will be included in the children's learning portfolios, together with learning stories, and these files, or portfolios, regularly go home with the families. Families, too, write learning stories from home, often in the home language, to e-mail to family in other countries. Families write comments in the files and for many children this record of their learning journey becomes their favourite book, even some time after they have left the kindergarten.

The interweaving of learning and teaching

The ICT, the documentation and the dialogue are the bridges between teaching and learning; they reflect the responsive and reciprocal relationships between the children and teachers, and they enhance relationship with the families. Children, too, are taking photographs and dictating stories about their learning:

> Children will often come looking for us now, won't they, to write their story . . . They'll say, 'Can you come and sit with me 'cos I've got to tell you my story' (Ramsey *et al.*, 2006, p.42).

In a 2005 report (Ramsey *et al.*, 2005) the teachers comment:

> The integration of ICT into teaching and learning has meant a quantum leap in the teachers' technology skills. This kind of upskilling takes time, patience, and

support from others. Some expected difficulties, however, did not arise. The children's files, as well as the photocopier, laminator, and printer, all became accessible to the children. As the children took on more responsibility, both for their files and for some aspects of their technology, (we) have been impressed by the children's respect and care for the new artefacts in their educational lives (pp.29–30).

The teachers began to add one-page teachers' stories to the front of the children's files. These told a little of the teacher's background and interests, and included some photographs. These became a great catalyst for dialogue with families and with teachers. A story in the final report (p.11) describes the families as teachers as well:

Simran's mother brought in photos from home. These photos generated much conversation and enabled us to deepen our relationship not only with Simran, but with her family too. Other families watched as we went through the photos and a few days later they too brought in their family pictures to share. This spiralling effect enabled many of the families to share their home life with us, giving us an invaluable insight into their unique lives. The parents became teachers.

Documentation and assessment

The teachers began to debrief for about 20 minutes at the end of the day, discussing the children's learning and planning together who will document what. In their discussions, they comment that:

We might notice that we're talking about the same children all the time. We now think about the other 20, and what's happening with them. Now, when we've written a learning story and we've printed it off and put it in the child's portfolio, we put a tick beside their name. At the same time we copy the story into their digital portfolio.

Planning

The teachers began to put the documentation onto the walls, enhancing their planning strategies and extending ideas and themes in collaboration with the children and their families. Two-sided theme boards on wheels were useful for this, as a number of themes – bead-work, mosaics, birdhouses at the carpentry table and superheroes, for example – would be developing at any one time. These later developed into planning stories and stories of interest (such as in Figure 8.2).

Key points

1. The weaving of the curriculum principles through each of the five strands of outcome is described in three ways:
    - the goals, which describe the teaching and learning environment
    - documentation and assessment
    - planning.
2. The goals emphasise participation. Each goal begins with the phrase 'Children experience an environment where . . .' or 'Children and families experience an environment where . . .'.
3. Assessment practices can prohibit, weaken, support or strengthen a curriculum so the Te Whāriki approach includes an assessment approach that enhances children's opportunities to learn.
4. Research and resource development for assessment of learning, underpinned by Te Whāriki, accompanied the development of the curriculum.
5. Assessments are written as stories of learning in familiar contexts and recognise the complex nature of learning.
6. As learning stories became more embedded in the culture of early childhood settings, it became increasingly obvious that a different process for planning was critical. The curriculum filter of noticing, recognising, responding, recording and revisiting became the key to effective planning.

Reflective questions

- Read Figure 8.1 (Kellen's Love for bracelets) again. Notice that the analysis of the learning has a dual focus: the subject (in this case, the mathematics) and the learning dispositions (in this case the persistence and the self-direction). Think of an episode of learning and teaching that you know well. How might you analyse the learning in these two ways?
- Read the planning example again:
    - What aspirations for children are apparent here?

 - Which learning lens is of most interest to you and why is this? Reflect on other examples of this lens from your own experience. How would you write a learning story about it?
 - In what ways did the planning look back and look forward, to include the continuity and progress over time?
■ Consider a sustained teaching and learning activity or project with young children. Choose some of the following reflective questions, in collaboration with other teachers involved:
 - How did it all start?
 - What learning was happening here?
 - How was this interest sustained?
 - How did we encourage complexity?
 - What supported continuity?
 - What are our thoughts about opportunities and possibilities for the child?
 - What surprised us?
 - Who were the planners?
 - What were the outside or community influences?
 - What shifts in our practice have we experienced?
 - Can we make links to theory and research?
 - How does this reflect and inform our beliefs about wise teaching?
 - What might we do differently next time?
■ Think about your assessment practice:
 - Who is the audience?
 - How does the assessment practice make the learning and the strengthening of learning, visible to the teachers, children and families?
 - What outcomes are assessed and what outcomes that you value are invisible in this assessment?
 - In what ways does the documentation build and strengthen the children's sense of themselves as a competent learner?
 - What opportunities are there for the children, families and teachers to revisit the learning?

References

Carr, M. (1998a) *Assessing Children's Experiences in Early Childhood: Final Report to the Ministry of Education*. Wellington: Ministry of Education.
Carr, M. (1998b) *Assessing Children's Experiences in Early Childhood: Three Videos and a Workshop Booklet for Practitioners*. Wellington: NZCER Press.

Carr, M. (2005) Changing the lens: sociocultural curriculum and research in early childhood in New Zealand. In B. Webber (ed.), *The Herbison Lectures 1999–2004* (pp.35–58). Wellington: NZCER Press.

Carr, M., Lee, W. and Jones, C. (2004, 2007 2009) *Kei Tua o Te Pae. Assessment for Learning: Early Childhood Exemplars*. Books 1–20. Wellington: Learning Media.

Drummond, M.-J. (2008) Assessment and values: a close and necessary relationship. In S. Swaffield (ed.), *Unlocking Assessment: Understanding for Reflection and Application* (pp.3–19). London: Routledge.

Greeno, J. G., Collins, A. M. and Resnick, L. B. (1996) Cognition and learning. In D. C. Berliner and R. C. Calfree (eds), *Handbook of Educational Psychology* (pp.15–46). New York: Simon and Schuster and London: Prentice Hall.

Guba, E. and Lincoln, Y. (1989) *Fourth Generation Evaluation*. Newbury Park, CA: Sage.

Hill, D. (2001) Passion, power and planning in the early childhood centre. The first years: Nga Tau Tuatahi. *New Zealand Journal of Infant and Toddler Education*, 3(2), 10–13.

Ramsey, K., Breen, J., Sturm, J., Lee, W. and Carr, M. (2005) Roskill South Kindergarten Centre of Innovation. In A. Meade (ed.), *Catching the Waves: Innovation in Early Childhood Education* (pp.25–30). Wellington: NZCER Press.

Ramsey, K., Breen, J., Sturm, J., Lee, W. and Carr, M. (2006) *Strengthening Learning and Teaching Using ICT. Final Report to Ministry of Education*. Wellington: NZCER Press.

Ramsey, K., Lee, W., Carr, M., and Hatherly, A. (2003; 2nd ed. in press) Te Whāriki and assessment: a case study of teacher change. In J. Nuttall (ed.) *Weaving Te Whāriki: Aotearoa's Early Childhood Curriculum Document in Theory and Practice*. Wellington: NZCER Press.

Rogoff, B. (1990) *Apprenticeship in Thinking: Cognitive Development in a Social Context*. Oxford and New York: Oxford University Press.

Wells, G. (1999) *Dialogic Inquiry: Towards a Sociocultural Practice and Theory of Education*. New York: Cambridge University Press.

9 | Teachers as researchers

From England, Jenny Woodbridge writes:

> Over a number of years Early Excellence has been privileged to work with early childhood educators from New Zealand to host conferences, seminars and professional education sessions focused on sharing the theory and pedagogy of Te Whāriki and the translation of the New Zealand curriculum into practice. The impact of this association has been significant and enabled Local Authorities, schools and individual practitioners to reflect deeply about the importance of building a curriculum focussed on nurturing children's learning dispositions and developing assessment and planning practices that acknowledge the importance of looking closely at children's learning and documenting this process through the creation of 'learning stories'. This relationship with New Zealand early childhood educators has promoted deeper reflection and understanding of children's learning and enabled clearer understanding in translating the Early Years Foundation Stage curriculum into practice.

It was clear from the very beginning that Te Whāriki was very different from a more traditional curriculum. It prioritised learning dispositions and working theories as outcomes, and gave teachers the responsibility for weaving the curriculum content into their programmes. From 1996 the government provided generous professional education for its implementation. In 1994, Maggie Haggerty and Pat Hubbard in their report of a research-based trial of the draft Te Whāriki guidelines in five early childhood centres identified a number of factors that had helped early childhood centres to use the guidelines. These were:

■ having a degree of familiarity with the document, particularly understanding the curriculum approach underpinning the guidelines.

- taking an 'adaptive' rather than an 'adoptive' approach. The notion of curriculum as tightly prescribed is rejected in Te Whāriki's approach. 'The concept of Te Whāriki, or an early childhood programme as weaving, implies there is no set way to develop a programme' (Carr and May, 1993b, p.129). Some participants wanted a recipe to follow and, although they knew this was not a workable approach, they did not know how to approach the task differently.
- having outside facilitators encouraged an adaptive approach.
- having time for reflection, planning and evaluation and being able to engage with the guidelines (pp.93–94).

Factors that assisted this process were a centre culture that accepted the need for ongoing change, a manageable workload, a high staff : child ratio, small group sizes, qualified staff, staff stability, supportive leadership and a view of the teacher as learner and researcher.

The implementation of Te Whāriki was later supported for 7 years from 2003 to 2007 by the Centre of Innovation action research programme, exemplified by the case studies in the previous five chapters. Furthermore, when assessment practices were developed, further professional education programmes supported the new assessment-for-learning resource, *Kei Tua o te Pae* (Carr *et al.*, 2004, 2007, 2009), introduced in earlier chapters. Some of these programmes and opportunities are outlined in this chapter, and we will argue that professional support is important if a curriculum approach is to be able to respond to and experiment with different environments, opportunities and times. From 2010 the two major curriculum and assessment professional development programmes were severely diminished by budget cuts and in 2009 the Centre of Innovation programme was ended. New professional development programmes are targeted towards centres in low-participating communities and centres that have been designated as of poor quality by the Education Review Office (which regularly evaluates all licenced early childhood centres and schools) and the Ministry of Education. Some national early childhood professional education remains, and this chapter gives a case study of one professional education programme, drawing on the work of the educational leadership project (ELP). Information on the ELP professional learning programme is available at http://www.elp.co.nz. A description of ELP as a case study (see Lee, 2008) uses the principles of Te Whāriki as a framework and outlines the purpose of the professional education as four Ps: passion (holism), pedagogy (relationships), positivity (empowerment) and participation (community).

Passion (holism)

Teachers' passions are nurtured in a setting that takes account of the holistic nature of learning. In the past the focus of professional learning requirements has been on both 'individual needs' and 'centre needs'. This deficit view is incompatible with the principles of Te Whāriki. Just as we emphasise the dispositions, knowledge and working theories that children have, so too should we look closely at how we enact this with adults in an early childhood setting. ELP's experience suggests this is best achieved when professional learning starts from a teacher's position of strength and builds on it. Finding out what teachers are passionate about and nurturing the passion is powerful, as we saw in the quote from Csikszentmihalyi (1997, p.158) in Chapter 6, on the apparent consequence, for some adults, of their tremendous interest and 'unquenchable curiosity' as children. Our role, then, is to find the ways in which we can nurture these passions and interests in order to 'provide the opportunities for them to grow and result in a creative life' (p.182). People are drawn to the enthusiasm, passion and energy of others. It has been our experience that teachers want to participate in professional education that promotes teacher innovation, persistence and celebration. Kent Peterson and Terrence Deal (1998, p.29) illustrate this aspect of organisational culture when they describe staff who

> have a shared sense of purpose – where they pour their hearts into the children and their teaching . . . where the informal network of storytellers, heroes and heroines provides a social web of positive information, support and history.

This teaches us that organisational culture is important for nurturing passion.

Most of us spend more time with the adults and children we work with than with those we love most in our lives – our partners, our husbands, our children and our best friends. Given this reality, it is vital that we create learning spaces and organisational cultures that nurture everyone, adults and teachers as well as children. The foundation of effective and sustained professional learning is a strong and positive organisational culture based on passion. People may forget what you say to them but they never forget how you make them feel.

One of the key strategies we have used to develop this sense of belonging and collegiality is to connect 'fish philosophy' with Te Whāriki. John Yokoyama developed the fish philosophy as an organisational culture in his place of work, a fish market (Yokoyama and Michelli, 2004). It led to greatly increased employee morale and this energised the work environment. This philosophy (Crother, 2004; Lundin, 2000) has a strong resonance with Te Whāriki. The four key ideas in fish philosophy are 'play', 'be there', 'choose your attitude' and 'make a difference'. These can be strongly linked to the four principles of Te Whāriki. The first principle of Te Whāriki, holism, is also about recognising the whole person and to be playful in the work environment. This idea recognises that people are drawn to play and are often energised by playfulness. We know that many of the large successful corporations like Apple, Google and Microsoft have workspaces that encourage and support playfulness. Play is not just an activity; it is a state of mind that brings new energy and sparks creativity (Lundin *et al.*, 2002; Lundin, 2000) as exemplified in Figure 9.1.

This playfulness can be about focus and finding flow. Mihaly Csikszentmihalyi (1996, 1997), whose work on creativity and on the feelings of flow or being in the moment, where skills and challenge are in balance, gives another view of this important notion of being playful. Playfulness is seeing that the ideas of work and play are interdependent and both support the notion of strengthening curiosity and creativity in adults as well as children. This sense of belonging and collegiality, if generated in an early childhood setting between the teachers and adults, will flow through to the children.

Carlina Rinaldi describes her holistic view, which has much in common with Te Whāriki, when she writes:

> Those who participate in the educational process, in fact bring their own growth and development into play, and do this on the basis of their own expectations and their own plans. There is a constant relational reciprocity between those who educate and those who are educated, between those who teach and those who learn. There is participation, passion, compassion, emotion. There is aesthetics; there is change. In this sense, I would like to mention the value of play, of fun, of emotions, of feelings, which we recognize as essential elements of any authentic cognitive and educational process. Learning thus becomes a value because of its force in creating a synthesis of the individual and his or her context, in an affective relationship between those who learn and that which is being learned, a relationship filled with emotion, curiosity and humour (2006, p.141).

Ken Robinson and Lou Aronica, in their book *The Element: How Finding Your Passion Changes Everything* (2009) note:

Guinea pig stories

Monty really loves the guinea pigs! I had such a lovely time with him today watching him interact with them. Snowflake was making little squeaky noises. "She's talking," Monty said, then he tipped his ear towards her and started interpreting her guinea pig talk into English. I thought this was very funny and very clever! Snowflake had some amazing stories to tell!

What did I discover about Monty today?

Monty is so playful, he has a wonderful imagination and is a fabulous storyteller. Let's look for opportunities to encourage him in his storytelling. I think he would enjoy doing some digital storytelling because he is very interested in the laptop.

Figure 9.1 Guinea pig stories

Written by Julie

The world is changing faster than ever in our history. Our best hope for the future is to develop a new paradigm of human capacity to meet a new era of human existence. We need to evolve a new appreciation of nurturing human talent along with an understanding of how talent expresses itself differently in every individual. We need to create environments – in our schools, in our workplaces, and in our public offices – where every person is inspired to grow creatively. We need to make sure that all people have the chance to do what they should be doing, to discover the Element in themselves and in their own way (p.xiii).

Robinson and Aronica go on to describe individuals who, by following their passions, achieved high levels of satisfaction, nurturing and further igniting their motivation. In these authors' view the element has two main features and there are two conditions for being in it. The features are aptitude and passion. The conditions are attitude and opportunity. The sequence goes something like this: 'I (can) get it (aptitude); I love it (passion); I want it (attitude); Where is it? (opportunity)' (2006, p.22).

It is in settings where teachers and practitioners have built a strong organisational culture, seeing themselves as a group of leaders who are working at being the best they can be, that such passion can flourish.

Pedagogy (relationships)

The pedagogy of relationships involves promoting close collaboration and reflection in a safe environment. In the words of Vivian Gussin Paley (1995), 'Any classroom – I know the kindergarten best – should develop into a close-knit community of people who care deeply about each other'. Professional education is not just a matter of describing or modelling good practice. A considerable element of trust and confidence is needed before teachers are prepared to question their thinking, risk failure and make significant changes. Professional education strategies that work to strengthen these attitudes include networking opportunities, encouraging teacher exchanges and visiting other centres. Vital to this is the ability to listen. Carlina Rinaldi (2006, p.65) describes in depth the pedagogy of listening, pointing out that:

> Listening is not easy. It requires deep awareness and at the same time a suspension of our judgements and above all our prejudices; it requires openness to change. It demands that we have clearly in mind the value of the unknown and that we are able to overcome the sense of emptiness and precariousness that we experience whenever our certainties are questioned.

This describes the depth of listening required to build a strong, resilient community of learners. The concept of the project facilitator becoming a critical friend of the teachers in a centre or setting is also a key element of

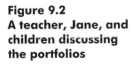

**Figure 9.2
A teacher, Jane, and
children discussing
the portfolios**

professional education focussing on pedagogy. A project facilitator
works as a critical friend to establish a strong respectful and reciprocal
relationship over time. Visits from the project facilitator can provide
fabulous learning strategies when time is given to observing the
programme, modelling practice (for example, writing learning stories),
talking to staff (sometimes individually) and working alongside the
teachers.

The provision of retreats, where staff take time out from the busy life of
teaching in a centre and spend time in dialogue with other teachers, is also
a powerful component of effective professional education that builds
relationships. Rinaldi (2006, p.76) refers to the notion of 'transformational
dialogue', providing an opportunity for these discussions and debates to
transform relationships and in turn transform the identity of the individuals as well as the wider group.

At a recent retreat Kerry shared her reflections of her journey:

Who would have thought Taupo had this 'secret', hidden away for opportunities
like this. What a perfect treat . . . I love the serenity of its environment as it
promotes thinking, creativity, peaceful existence, generation of a community of
learners in ECE. I feel like this group has had, over the years, relational
experiences but those really only existed at the top of each learning establishment
(e.g. head teachers and centre managers). As leadership is a team journey, this
learning establishment can now enjoy extending those opportunities to the rest of
the team's members, creating a much larger contingent of leaders in the group.
Planning for revisiting these experiences is powerful and provides excitement for

the possibilities that could lie ahead, and I think they should, for the growth and development of all of us. I would like to be involved in or be part of a leadership group that can collaborate on ideas and resources and help create a brighter future with our learning community. I do feel quite positive that this group could grow closer together and I hope it does.

Positivity (empowerment)

Positivity encourages each participant to take an active role in their learning and research and to own issues and create solutions. One of the critical aspects of successful professional learning is to take a credit rather than a deficit approach in order to support the learning repertoires and dispositions of children and adults. For example, Bishop *et al.* (2003, p.22) state: 'If the image we hold for Māori children or indeed any children . . . is one of deficits, then our principles and practices will reflect this, and we will thereby perpetuate the education crisis'. In our view, effective professional education asks teachers to focus on their strengths and to build a strong and positive culture of learning in their place of work.

Positivity is encouraged by focusing on a research question, on an area where the team wishes to make improvements and develop their strengths. Manageable and interesting action-based research projects have proved to be a powerful professional education strategy in achieving this.

Traditionally, research has been viewed as the realm of academics and as a painstaking, complex process taking several years to complete. But on its own, research simply means 'investigate, explore, inquire, examine' and this is what teachers do every day as they work in an early childhood centre. As practising teachers they are making an invaluable contribution in determining an area of focus for education, and then they investigate, explore, analyse, reflect and review that area through a research question. The value of a research process in ECE professional learning community is exemplified in the Ministry of Education Centre of Innovation programme *Pathways to the Future: Ngā Huarahi Arataki* (2002). This includes the following vision for Centres of Innovation by the year 2012:

We are constantly challenging and extending the depth of knowledge within the ECE sector. Centres of Innovation foster research and development in the ECE sector and reflect New Zealand's heritage of ingenuity and innovation. The centres capitalise on the experience of those most likely to produce the best ideas – the people working in ECE services. The programme sees ECE teachers combining their skills with the complementary skills of researchers. The regular change in the research cycle allows the exploration, documentation and sharing of a diverse range of skills and practices that continues to extend the effectiveness of teaching and learning (Ministry of Education 2002, p.15).

A research question focus is developed as an integral part of the ELP programme, and action research has been an integral part of the project since its inception. This has, over the period of the project, deepened and proved to have an enormous potential to build research capability in the early childhood sector. The practice of teachers as researchers is now well established and is empowering teachers within settings while fostering a sense of positivity. To build upon this work, we invited teams who had been on the project for 1 or 2 years to deepen their research study and to consider the question: 'How can this feature of our practice be documented in order to contribute to the professional education of other centres?' ELP employed an experienced academic researcher to help teachers define research questions and to devise methodologies for exploring these questions. In both these roles the professional knowledge of the teachers is paramount. The planned outcome of this part of the project was to support teachers in presenting their work at national conferences and eventually to publish their findings. As a consequence, several project facilitators and a number of teachers have published their work since joining the ELP. This research helps expand the theoretical knowledge of and basis for professional education and it provides stronger links between the academic and practical spheres of professional education. Early years teachers have also researched and published from the Ministry of Education's TLRI programme (see acknowledgement on p.xi).

In order to create a community of learners and leaders that is positive, eloquent, persuasive, strong, energetic and willing to debate and contribute to the community of practice, everyone needs to be able to find their voice and to know that their contributions are valued.

Taking a positive approach also means seeing a leader in everyone. If within a community there are members who believe they are not and cannot be leaders, then an exploration of the work of Carol Dweck is helpful. Dweck (2000, 2006) has the potential to transform every person's life by recognising that our future growth is in our own hands. In her

Shared leadership in action

Today, as I watched Alex, Jordan and Cameron working alongside each other I saw shared leadership in action.The three friends were busily working in the sandpit together when Alex said, "Okay Jordan, I'm finished!  Its your turn to choose the game now." "Yay," said Jordan."Let's play racing cars now. Everyone get your cars out." "Cool, and then it will be my turn to choose the game for everyone," Cam called out as he followed his friends to find his car.

I sat in awe as the trio went about their day deeply immersed in a culture of shared leadership. Many hours of negotiating and respecting each others' ideas had obviously led them to a place where they each felt empowered to contribute. Goose bumps ran over my skin as I soaked up the meaningfulness of their relationship and thought about the story I would sit down to write in reflection of their learning.

As we look towards a move to school for Alex and Jordan this year (and of course Cam in the future) it is clear to see that they will embark on their journeys with a sound understanding of the Key Competencies that support the primary curriculum. Relating to Others, for example, states that . . . "Students who relate well to others are open to new learning and able to take different roles in different situations. They are aware of how their words and actions affect others. They know when it is appropriate to compete and when it is appropriate to co-operate. By working effectively together, they can come up with new approaches, ideas and ways of thinking."

What wise, resourceful and leaderful young men you will no doubt be in the future.

Figure 9.3 Shared leadership in action

Written by Melissa

words: 'I have always been deeply moved by outstanding achievement, especially in the face of adversity, and saddened by wasted potential' (p.ix). We must ensure that every teacher, child and parent is open to all the possible selves that they can be. This notion of positivity is as important in our assessment of children as it is in teacher appraisal.

Participation (community)

Being advocates for children and families, and articulating viewpoints and theoretical ideas about teaching and learning are features of a professional educator with a strong sense of community participation and knowledge of pedagogical practice. Many enter teaching because of their strong altruistic goals to make a difference in children's lives and their real sense of purpose. As Michael Fullan (2006) has said:

> School leaders with moral purpose seek to make a difference in the lives of students. They are concerned about . . . raising the achievement of – and closing the gap between – high performing and lower-performing students.

Stephen Covey discusses the importance of the personal voice and its significance to all individuals. He says: 'There is a deep, innate, almost inexpressible yearning within each one of us to find our voice in life' (Covey, 2004, pp.5–6). Workshops can open up opportunities for teachers to find their voice and for centre facilitators and lead teachers to become effective leaders of the professional education in their settings. Some of the key ideas that might be covered in such workshops could include:

- examining leadership
- team building
- adult learning
- facilitation of groups
- exploring the formulation of focus areas and research questions for professional education
- developing an understanding and use of action research methods
- establishing professional learning communities
- building strong and positive learning cultures
- debating assessment for learning issues
- evaluating and reflecting on professional education progress and issues in the centre.

All teachers are given an opportunity to share their work and to articulate their practice in the professional learning community. These opportunities strengthen the early childhood sector and sustain professional education.

End of year presentations have also facilitated participation. At the end of the project year ELP holds a forum for centre facilitators and their teams to present their journey and the outcomes of the year's work. This is an exciting, challenging and rewarding time for all those who are involved in professional education. It is a celebration of the year's work and a chance to share successes, learn from others and develop deeper participation in the early childhood community.

We have focused on just four elements of successful professional education in an early childhood setting linked to the principles of Te Whāriki. These are summarised in Table 9.1.

In any early childhood setting there will be many leaders. Schlechty (1997) provides a useful analogy:

> Shared leadership . . . is less like an orchestra, where the conductor is always in charge, and more like a jazz band, where leadership is passed around . . . depending on what the music demands at the moment and who feels most moved by the spirit to express the music.

Each and every teacher and educator can make a difference, and no one says this more eloquently than Mahatma Gandhi (Dutt Misha and Gupta, 2008, p.36): 'A small body of determined spirits, fired by an unquenchable faith in their mission, can alter the course of history.'

Key points

1. Implementation of Te Whāriki was supported by a government-funded professional education programme focused on Te Whāriki for 10 years.
2. Teacher research on Te Whāriki and related early childhood teaching and learning topics was supported for 7 years from 2003 to 2007 by the action research Centre of Innovation programme and continues to be supported by the action research TLRI programme.
3. An early childhood resource on assessment for learning in early childhood, entitled '*Kei Tua o te Pae – Assessment for Learning*' (Carr *et al.*, 2004, 2007, 2009), was published by the Ministry of Education. It

Table 9.1 Elements of effective professional education

Principles of Te Whāriki	Relationships	Holistic	Empowerment	Community
Elements	Pedagogy of relationships: promoting close collaboration and reflection in a safe environment	Passion: nurturing participants passions in a setting that takes account of the holistic nature of learning and research	Positivity: encourage each participant to take an active role in their learning and research, to own issues and to create solutions	Politics: place value on everyone in the wider community being involved. Nurturing democracy and issues of justice
In practice	Deep listening Relationships Critical friends Community of learners	Holistic Powerful culture Playfulness Kindness Strong centre culture	Focus on strengths and interests: Competent learners Puzzling over uncertainty	Advocacy Leadership Making a difference Involving everyone in the professional education
Professional education strategies	Cluster groups Retreats Networking Teacher swap Visiting centres In-centre visits (strength of relationship with project facilitator)	Establishing the culture of the place four simple strategies linked to the principles of Te Whāriki (play, be there, choose your attitude and make a difference)	Setting own research focus or project focus Start from a strength base Write journals and learning logs	Sharing and contributing Work at workshops Involving the wider community Articulating your practice End of year presentation

was supported by professional education that ran for 5 years and provided in depth, in-centre professional learning opportunities across the nation.

4. The Te Whāriki approach can provide frameworks for professional education and action research programmes that connect the principles of Te Whāriki to programmes for adults in the following ways:
    (i)   Holism. Teachers' passions are nurtured in a setting that takes account of the holistic nature of learning.
    (ii) Relationships. At the heart of all programmes for both children and teachers is a pedagogy of relationships.
    (iii) Empowerment. Positivity encourages each participant to take an active role in their learning and research, and to own issues, and create solutions. A credit rather than a deficit approach supports the learning repertoires and dispositions of adults as well as children and families.
    (iv) Community. Being an advocate for children and families and articulating viewpoints and theoretical ideas about teaching and learning are features of a professional educator with a strong sense of community participation and sound pedagogical practice.
5. Shared and distributed leadership is an important key to building a strong and powerful learning community where all teachers feel that they have the power to make a difference.
6. Workshops that start with the idea of teachers as researchers will provide opportunities for teachers to:
    – find their voice
    – become professional education leaders in their settings
    – share their own work and articulate their practice
    – reflect on their professional education journey.

Reflective questions

■ Read Figure 9.1 (Guinea pig stories) again. This story includes a number of features that a professional education or teacher education workshop might take as a focus: interpretation, playfulness, imagination and storytelling.
    – How do teachers become more skilled at listening into and interpreting young children's thoughts, especially those who cannot yet articulate their interests, passions and concerns?

- How do teachers become more skilled at encouraging young children to watch out, interpret and care for others, especially those who cannot yet articulate their interests, passions and concerns? (See Figure 2.1 (Kindness of a friend) in Chapter 2.)
- What might playful teachers look like and how do they get better at playfulness? Why might we want teachers to be playful?
- In what ways do teachers need to be imaginative? How can this quality be practised and strengthened?
- How can teachers become fabulous storytellers?
- How can teachers become skilled digital storytellers, using twenty-first century digital technology to good advantage in order to provide assessment for learning and an early childhood education for children that communicates and collaborates with families and is also empowering, relational, and holistic?

■ Read Figure 9.3 (Shared leadership in action) again. It describes an episode of shared leadership in action in an early childhood centre. This story includes a number of features that a professional education or teacher education workshop might take as a focus. Reflect on some of these:

- What example of adults negotiating and respecting each others' ideas comes to mind? What strategies and provocations were effective? How could they have been improved? In what ways was the purpose important (as something that everyone wanted to improve)?
- What features of a culture of shared leadership at your centre or in your teacher education class do you value?
- In what ways will shared leadership expertise and dispositions, such as those described as relating to others in the New Zealand school curriculum (see Chapter 10) assist children to become good learners at school? Share specific examples that you know about. Explore the biographies of successful researchers, conservationists, scientists, teachers, artists and Nobel prize winners: what leadership and learning dispositions were evident in their stories? Who are your heroes?
- What might a wise and resourceful leader and citizen look like in your country? How can early childhood education start children off on this journey?

References

Bishop, R., Berryman, M., Tiakiwai, S. and Richardson, C. (2003) *Te Kotahitanga: The Experiences of Year 9 and 10 Māori Students in Mainstream Classrooms.* Report to the Ministry of Education. Wellington: Ministry of Education.

Covey, S. R. (2004) *The 8th Habit: From Effectiveness to Greatness.* London: Simon and Schuster.

Crother, C. (2004) *Catch: A Fishmongers Guide to Greatness.* San Francisco, CA: Berrett-Koehler.

Csikszentmihalyi, M. (1997) *Finding Flow: The Psychology of Engagement with Everyday Life.* New York: Basic Books.

Dutt Mishra, A. and Gupta, R. (2008) *Inspiring Thoughts of Mahatma Gandhi: Ghandi in Daily Life.* New Delhi: Concept.

Dweck C. S. (2000) *Self-Theories: Their Role in Motivation, Personality, and Development.* New York: Psychology Press.

Dweck, C. S. (2006) *Mindset: The New Psychology of Success.* New York: Random House.

Fullan, M. (2006) *Turnaround Leadership.* Thousand Oaks, CA: Corwin Press.

Haggerty, M. and Hubbard, P. (1994) Te Whāriki trial: five Wellington centres work on an agreed basis for curriculum in early childhood services in Aotearoa New Zealand. Unpublished report to the Ministry of Education.

Harris, A. and Lambert, L. (2003) *Building Leadership Capacity for School Improvement.* Maidenhead: Open University Press.

Kemmis, S. and McTaggart, R. (2000) Participatory action research. In N. K. Denzin and Y. S. Lincoln (eds), *Handbook of Qualitative Research*, 2nd edn (pp.567–605). London: Sage.

Lee, W. (2008) ELP: empowering the leadership in professional development communities. *European Early Childhood Education Research Journal*, 16(1), 95–106.

Lundin, S. C. (2000) *Fish Omnibus: A Remarkable Way to Boost Morale and Improve Results.* London: Hodder and Stoughton.

Lundin S. C., Christensen J. and Paul, H. (2002) *Fish Tales*. New York: Hyperion.

Ministry of Education (2002) *Pathways to the Future: Ngā Huarahi Arataki.* Wellington: Learning Media.

Mitchell, L. and Cubey, P. (2003) Characteristics of professional development linked to enhanced pedagogy and children's learning in early childhood settings: best evidence synthesis. Retrieved 25 August 2012 from http://www.educationcounts.govt.nz/publications/series/2515/5955.

Paley, V. G. (1995) Lessons of Room 284. *Chicago Tribune Magazine*, 25 June, pp. 12–19 and 28–29.

Peterson, K. D. and Deal, T. E. (1998) How leaders influence culture of schools. *Educational Leadership*, 56(1), 28–30.

Rinaldi, C. (2006) *In Dialogue with Reggio Emilia: Listening, Researching and Learning.* London and New York: Routledge.

Robinson, K. and Aronica, L. (2009) *The Element: How Finding Your Passion Changes Everything*. London: Penguin.

Schlechty, P. C. (1997) *Inventing Better Schools: An Action Plan for Educational Reform*. San Francisco: Jossey-Bass.

Yokoyama, J. and Michelli, J. (2004) *When Fish Fly: Lessons for Creating a Vital and Energized Workplace*. New York: Hyperion.

10 The future

From Denmark Stig Broström writes:

Since the last part of the 1990s, early childhood education and care in the Nordic countries has focused on the question of how to create and express a theory and practice which balances on the one hand the child-oriented tradition and, on the other, a goal-oriented curriculum approach. In this process Nordic researchers have communicated the core and soul of Te Whāriki. Several dimensions have inspired the field of preschool practice. First of all the fact that Te Whāriki goes beyond a technical understanding of education and curriculum by using a theoretical framework, namely a socio-cultural approach. More researchers and preschool teachers have been inspired with the ideas about doing documentation. Thus, the theory and method of learning stories has had a big influence.

The Te Whāriki approach has been described in this book as a curriculum and associated pedagogy that has social, cultural and educational core assumptions. We have attempted to 'take readers elsewhere . . . and, in so doing perhaps to make the educationally familiar a bit stranger', as Allan Luke says in an essay about exporting policy from one country to another (Luke, 2011, p.368). Luke commented that the curriculum stories from small countries 'are about cultural and governmental settlements, about durable historical, social, and cultural commitments to particular forms of education and, indeed, forms of life' (p.374). We have referred to some of those commitments and described the role of history, place and culture in the curriculum decisions that led to a national early childhood curriculum in Aotearoa New Zealand. Te Whāriki looks back and across, and also forward to aspirations for children, to the settlements to do with what we value as outcomes for children and how we might get there.

This chapter looks, briefly, forward as well, to the future in three further, interconnected ways at:

- opportunities and possibilities for the future as the Te Whāriki approach to teaching and learning responds to changes in economic and political climates
- the opportunities and possibilities for the Te Whāriki approach to influence the children's next stage of education, at school
- the power of teachers as researchers.

Opportunities and possibilities for the future as the Te Whāriki approach to teaching and learning responds to changes in economic and political climates

What will sustain the Te Whāriki curriculum in Aotearoa New Zealand and the experiments in recontextualising educational principles and practices elsewhere? We return to some of the themes in this book to hazard a guess at the answer to this question. For our country, it will mean remembering our cultural history and holding our nerve – holding onto and continuing to advocate the relational, holistic, empowerment and community values in Te Whāriki – while at the same time being courageous and imaginative enough to experiment in response to children's initiatives as well as to shifting economic and political climates. As Stig Broström writes in the comment that opens this chapter, there are balances to be struck. The theoretical underpinning of Te Whāriki – going beyond the technical – will assist practitioners to articulate their practice in response to global interests in standardisation and measurements of added value. James Greeno (1997, p.9) asked the following question and this book has asked it as well:

> Should we consider the major goals and outcomes of learning primarily as collections of sub skills or as successful participation in socially organised activity and the development of students' identities as learners?

The assumption that assessment has a central role in identity formation (Gipps, 2002; Carr and Lee, 2012) is now a key feature of the Te Whāriki approach and all the chapters of this book have included some examples of documentation that has the notion of learner identities in mind: learners who have well-practised repertoires of knowledge and are disposed to exploration, communication, well-being, contribution and belonging.

The opportunities and possibilities of the Te Whāriki approach to influence the children's next stage of education, at school

What happens when children go to school? When this national early childhood curriculum was being developed the early childhood sector in Aotearoa New Zealand was anxious about the possible 'schoolification' (Bennett, 2006; see also the quote by Sumison *et al.*, 2009, in Chapter 5) of early childhood: the 'push down' of achievement objectives, by levels, in subject areas. Traditionally, early childhood education has kept away from the school curriculum, often focusing on play. Bennett sees the school curriculum as a narrowing and fragmenting of the educational focus on subjects. The literature on 'preparation' and 'readiness' for school is extensive, as Sally Peters' work has illustrated (Peters, 2010). But, of course, children will go on to school from an early childhood provision: does the Te Whāriki approach have something to say about this aspect of the future? Once again, the history of events in Aotearoa New Zealand has become very relevant to this question, and some of the detail of this going to school history is recounted by Helen May (2011).

In 2007 a new school curriculum was published. The development discussions for this school curriculum looked closely at the previous school curriculum's array of essential skills. The curriculum developers in the Ministry had become alert to Organization for Economic Cooperation and Development work on key competencies (Rychen and Salganik, 2001, 2003). Advocates of early childhood were at the curriculum table while this curriculum was being developed, pressing for an alignment with Te Whāriki. In the final published document the school curriculum included five key competencies as a central component of student outcomes. These key competencies were aligned with the strands of Te Whāriki (see Figure 10.1). In effect, we felt, the Te Whāriki approach had pushed up into the school curriculum.

Both the early childhood sector and the school sector have begun to experiment with how this alignment might be implemented in practice. From 2006 to 2008 three teacher-researchers and two university-researchers researched together at Mangere Bridge Kindergarten on the

This diagram suggests how the tertiary competencies align with those of *Te Whāriki* and *The New Zealand Curriculum*:

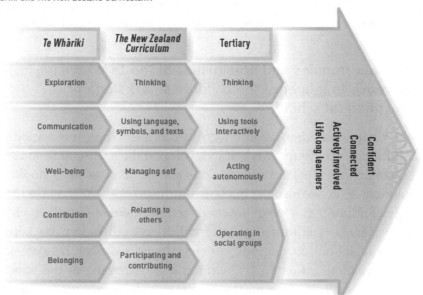

Figure 10.1 The key competencies: cross-sector alignment

sixth Centre of Innovation project to appear in this book. This two-session (afternoon and morning) kindergarten's community included 86 families with approximately 15 different cultural backgrounds. The aim was to support the transition from early childhood to school, and papers and a book were written by the teachers and their university colleagues (Hartley *et al.*, 2010, 2012). A comment in the 2012 book (p.89) said that the 2007 school curriculum provides a potential bridge to support children's learning across sectors but the strength of the bridge depends on the connections that are deliberately made by both early childhood and school teachers.

During this research project a number of deliberately designed activities and artefacts crossed the boundary between the kindergarten and the local schools. These included projects of mutual interest: a Welcome to School' DVD project and the establishment of an early childhood and primary links group where representatives from early childhood and school settings in the local community came together on a regular basis to discuss topics of mutual interest and pedagogy and practice in each setting. Earlier, the kindergarten children had taken cameras on school visits and photographed what was important to them, reminiscent of the research on children's voices by Clark and Moss (2011) referred to earlier. Portfolios of learning stories followed the children into school and became literacy and communication artefacts, as well as informing the teachers at school of the children's capabilities, interests and progress over time. In another research project with teachers at Taitoko Kindergarten (Clarkin-Phillips and Carr, 2009), transition folders were developed in which the children and the teachers together constructed a folder of favourite learning stories that exemplified each of the aligned domains of outcome in the school and the early childhood curriculum shown in Figure 10.1. This initiative was the outcome of consultation between the early childhood teachers and the local school teachers.

In Figure 10.2 Cathy, the teacher, comments on twenty-first century technology, acknowledges the ancestors and describes the learning dispositions for learning that will stay with you in this world.

The power of teachers as researchers

From California in the USA, Mark Whitney writes:

> I still tend to hold on to my old ideas because they have meaning and familiarity and a certain degree of comfort, but my visit to New Zealand's early childhood programs has opened my mind to new ways of solving problems. I simply cannot look at the world with my old set of lenses, and things look different now. In short, I have been deeply and profoundly provoked, and any professional discomfort I am feeling is certainly a good thing because I know it will lead me to new ways of (re)imagining my work.

Given the global trend towards standardisation and a narrowing of curriculum in schools, this re-imagining will also include the democratic experimentalism that Peter Moss writes about (2009) and the opportunities for professional development and practitioner research that will be needed to sustain it. Teachers as researchers are teachers as learners, curious about children's learning and uncertain of the outcome. Even small research projects that are initiated by a teaching team who are puzzling together over an aspect of their work can be a successful way to understand how a curriculum approach might be recontextualised in a new environment.

Policy initiatives implemented through the New Zealand government's strategic plan for early childhood education (Ministry of Education, 2002) in the last decade have had a considerable impact on raising levels of

Hold fast to the words of your ancestors

Kia mau ki ngā kupu ā ō tūpuna
Hold fast to the words of your ancestors

He kakano ahau, ruia mai i Rāngiatea
I am a seed, scattered from Rāngiatea

Tuari you notice Ava is using the iPad. I can see you are
interested, as our eyes connect, I realise how longingly you
are looking at this new tool. In your quiet, calm way you
make your wishes known to me, not so much with words,
and we understand each other. I invited you to join in with us.

I think your brain is a real thinking brain Tuari. I see a
strength and humility in you that enriches me every day
Tuari. As we learn and teach each other, at kindergarten, in
your quiet way you show me how you care for others, you
have an aura of peace about you that I and others enjoy.

I wonder about your tupuna Tuari, where you have come
from. I heard a whakataukī at the weekend that said "the
ancestors stand on my shoulders to keep my feet on the
ground." Your humility shows me your feet are on the
ground.

Here you are being curious, excited and courageous as you
try something new on the iPad. You are a great learner and
you are learning to take responsibility for your learning and

attempt some difficult tasks. I think your tupuna were courageous, curious and excited as they travelled the oceans on the great migration, settled in this land and supported each other in their whānau, hapū and iwi.

These dispositions for learning are the things that will stay with you in this world, passed down from your tupuna and into your future Tuari. I am privileged to learn from you and to teach you on part of that life long journey.

Figure 10.2 Kia mau ki ngā kupu ā ō tūpuna/Hold fast to the words of your ancestors

Written by Cathy

teacher qualifications and enhancing teachers' professional capabilities. In 2002 the government set out a staged plan for lifting the levels of qualifications, with the aim of attaining a 100 per cent qualified teaching workforce by 2012. Although this aim has been modified, the official target stands at 80 per cent of staff in teacher-led services as qualified teachers holding a 3-year early childhood teacher education qualification and registration certifying they are capable to teach.

In a longitudinal policy evaluation of the strategic plan from 2002 to 2007 Mitchell and Hogden (2008) found that there were large positive shifts on every indicator of teaching and learning practices (assessment, planning, evaluation and self review), as well as teachers' understanding of the Te Whāriki approach and relationships with parents in the early childhood setting. These were directly associated with the high and continuing take-up and use of Ministry of Education funded and published assessment and self-review resources, professional development, the Centres of Innovation action research dissemination and the employment of registered teachers. A clear message from the evaluation was that teachers' understanding of sociocultural theory had been enhanced, that teachers were better able to work with families' funds of knowledge (Gonzales *et al.*, 2005) and that the curriculum implementation had become more permeable – 'open to contribution from all comers' (Carr *et al.*, 2001, p.31). We hope that these discussions of the Te Whāriki approach will lead practitioners and teacher educators in Aotearoa New Zealand and other countries to explore their own practice in small local ways, to experiment in collaboration with their colleagues and their families and the children, and to consider, with Mark Whitney, new ways of (re)imagining their work.

References

Bennett, J. (2006) 'Schoolifying' early childhood education and care: accompanying pre-school into education. Unpublished paper. London: Institute of Education, University of London.

Carr, M. (2006) Learning dispositions and key competencies: a new curriculum continuity across the sectors? *Early Childhood Folio*, 10, 21–26.

Carr, M., Lowie, B., Gerrity, R., Jones, C., Lee, W. and Pohio, L. (2001) Democratic Learning and Teaching Communities: can assessment play a role? Keynote address. In *Proceedings of NZCER Annual Conference: Early Childhood Education for a Democratic Society*. Wellington: NZCER Press.

Gipps, C. (2002) Sociocultural Perspectives on Assessment. In G. Wells and G. Claxton (eds), *Learning for Life in the 21st Century: Sociocultural Perspectives on the Future of Education* (pp.73–83). Oxford: Blackwell.

Gonzales, N., Moll, L. C. and Amanti, C. (2005) *Funds of Knowledge: Theorizing Practices in Households, Communities and Classrooms*. Mahwah, NJ: Erlbaum.

Greeno, J. G. (1997) On claims that answer the wrong question. *Educational Researcher* 26(1), 5–17.

Hartley, C., Rogers, P., Smith, J. Peters, S. and Carr, M. (2010) Building relationships between early childhood and school: mutually interesting projects. In A. Meade (ed.), *Dispersing Waves: Innovation in Early Childhood Education* (pp.19–26). Wellington: NZCER Press.

Hartley, C., Rogers, P., Smith, J., Peters, S. and Carr, M. (2012) *Across the Border: A Community Negotiates the Transition from Early Childhood to Primary School*. Wellington: NZCER Press.

Luke, A. (2011) Generalizing across borders: policy and the limits of educational science. *Educational Researcher*, 40(8), 367–77.

Mitchell, L. and Hodgen, E. (2008) *Locality Based Evaluation of Pathways to the Future – Nga Huarahi Arataki* (Stage 1 report). Wellington: Ministry of Education.

Peters, S. (2010) Shifting the lens: reframing the view of learners and learning during the transition from early childhood education to school in New Zealand. In D. Jindal-Snape (ed.) *Educational Transitions: Moving Stories from Around the World* (pp.68–84). London: Routledge.

Rychen, D. S. and Salganik, L. H. (eds), (2001) *Defining and Selecting Key Competencies*. Gottingen: Hogrefe and Huber.

Rychen, D. S. and Salganik, L. H. (eds), (2003) *Key Competencies for a Successful Life and Well-Functioning Society*. Cambridge, MA: Hogrefe and Huber.

Sumison, J., Cheeseman, S., Kennedy, A., Barnes, S., Harrison, L. and Stonehouse, A. (2009) Insider perspectives on developing belonging, being and becoming: the early years learning framework for Australia. *Australasian Journal of Early Childhood*, 34(4), 4–13.

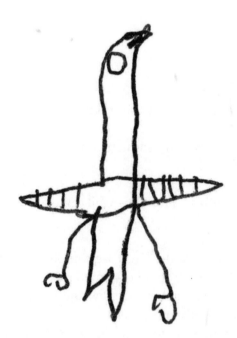

Glossary of Māori terms

ako Teaching and learning

Aotearoa Aotearoa is the most commonly used Māori name for New Zealand

aroha Compassion, empathy, sadness, love, affection

atawhai Caring for others

atua Guardian, god

E hoa mā – ka pai, kōtiro Friends – Well done girl

hapū Sub-tribe

harikoa Joy, happiness

He kōtiro kaha koe ki te ārahi You are a good leader (talking to a girl)

He tino iti te ao The world is a very small place

He waka eke noa 'A canoe to be used without restriction', can be an analogy for community ownership

He Whāriki Mātauranga mō ngā Mokopuna o Aotearoa Early Childhood Curriculum

iwi Tribe

Ka pai tō mahi Great work

kahikatea A tree endemic to Aotearoa New Zealand

Kaitiaki Teacher, guardian, trustee

Kei Tua o te Pae Beyond the horizon

kōhanga reo Language nest (total immersion Māori language educational settings for children 0–6 years) developed in the early 1980s by Māori to save the Māori language and culture from extinction

koro Grandfather

Kotahitanga Holistic development

Mana Status, authority, power

Mana aotūroa Exploration

Mana atua Well-being

Mana reo Communication

Mana Tamariki The name of a specific language nest (total immersion Māori language educational settings for children 0–6 years) in Palmerston North

Mana tangata Contribution

Mana whenua Belonging

Manaaki Hospitality, care for, look after

Manaakitanga The practice of the above (hospitality, caring for, looking after)

Māori The first settlers and indigenous people of Aotearoa New Zealand

Marae The traditional gathering place of the Māori extended family, the sub-tribe and the tribe. In the present day marae provide a place where Māori ways of being and doing are paramount. At marae Māori values and philosophies underpin activities. This way of being is witnessed in the way in which Māori farewell their dead (tangi). The marae is not reserved for Māori only but is an open space where non-Māori, including Pākehā, are welcome to share in Māori processes and protocols. Traditionally the space was an open courtyard but in the present day the term refers to all buildings and the land upon which they stand in the given area of the marae

Maui A demigod in Māori mythology

mihimihi Ceremonial greetings where participants take turns to acknowledge each other, their connections and the purpose for which they have gathered

moko Shortened form of mokopuna

mokopuna Grandchildren

Ngā 'The' plural

Ngā hononga Relationships

Ngā Huarahi Arataki Pathways to the future

ngā tikanga Māori Māori ways of doing, cultural practices, customs and rituals

Pākehā First European settlers and their descendants or non-Māori peoples whose ways of being and doing have been developed here in Aotearoa New Zealand over generations and are distinct to this environment

Paki ako Māori narratives of children's learning as developed by and for Te Kōhanga Reo o Mana Tamariki

Papa-tū-ā-nuku   The earth mother

pepehā   Tribal identity statement

pōhiri/pōwhiri   Formal traditional welcome ceremony

rangatira   Chiefs

Rangiātea   The spiritual homeland of Māori

rangimārie   Peace/calm

Ranginui   The sky father

reo   Language

Ruruku kai   Acknowledgements made before partaking of food

tamariki   Children

tangata   People

Tangata whenua   Tangata Whenua literally means 'people of the land'.
   It is a Māori term for the descendants of the first people to settle
   Aotearoa – New Zealand.
      Within an international context the term includes all first peoples
   or nations.
      Within a Māori context, tangata whenua are whānau (extended
   family groups), hapū (sub-tribes) and iwi (tribes) who have
   customary authority over an area that may include land and sea.
   That authority is held by first settlement of an area or by succeeding
   to an area through active occupation and negotiation with the first
   peoples. Customary authority is only exercised by certain groups
   within the boundaries of a certain area

taonga   Treasure

Tawhaki   One of the key characters in the Māori creation stories

Te   'The' singular

te ao Māori   The Māori world

Te Kōhanga Reo o Mana Tamariki   See Kōhanga Reo definition

Te Reo Maori   The Māori language

Te Tiriti o Waitangi   The Treaty of Waitangi

Te Whāriki   The early childhood curriculum has been envisaged as a
   whāriki, or mat, woven from the principles, strands and goals
   defined in this document. The whāriki concept recognises the
   diversity of early childhood education in Aotearoa New Zealand.
   Different programmes, philosophies, structures, and environments
   will contribute to the distinctive patterns of the whāriki

Tino ātaahua rāua   Those two are very beautiful

Tino rangatiratanga   Authority over their lives and resources

tuangi   New Zealand clam

tūpuna   Ancestor

waiata   Song

Waitangi   A township in the Bay of Islands, where the Treaty of Waitangi was signed in 1840

Whakamana   Empowerment

whakapapa   Genealogy, family tree

whakataukī   Proverb or saying

Whānau   Extended family, network of kin

Whanaungatanga   Staying connected with whānau

Whānau tangata   Family and community

whāriki   Woven mat

Index